Collins

need to know?

Horse & Pony Care

In association with
The British Horse Society

Collins

First published in 2006 by Collins
an imprint of
HarperCollins Publishers
77–85 Fulham Palace Road
London W6 8JB

www.collins.co.uk

Collins is a registered trademark of HarperCollins Publishers Limited

10 09 08 07 06
6 5 4 3 2 1

A catalogue record for this book is available from the British Library

Editor: Heather Thomas
Designer: Rolando Ugolini
Series design: Mark Thomson
Photographers: Rolando Ugolini and Margaret Linington-Payne
Front cover photograph: A.Inden/Zefa/Corbis
Back cover photographs: Rolando Ugolini

Based on material from *The British Horse Society's
Complete Horse & Pony Care*

ISBN-13: 978 0 00 722589 7
ISBN-10: 0 00 722589 X

Colour reproduction by Colourscan, Singapore
Printed and bound by Printing Express Ltd, Hong Kong

Contents

1 Choosing a horse

The decision to acquire a horse or pony is one of the biggest that you will ever make, and therefore it is very important to consider all the issues involved before you even think of buying one. Try to resist the temptation to 'fall in love' with a horse and then resolve that you must have it. Before you do anything else, you must decide what sort of horse is suitable for you. Look at and ride several horses and do as much checking as you possibly can before you part with your hard-earned money.

Buying a horse

The golden rule when buying a horse is that the onus is always on the purchaser to ensure that the horse is what they believe it to be and that it is suitable. This is known as *caveat emptor* – let the buyer beware. You should never take the seller's word for it when they say that the horse is sound, fit, healthy and suitable for you.

Ask yourself
- Can I afford to own my own horse?
- Do I have time to own a horse?
- Will I keep the horse at livery or look after it myself at home?
- Is my riding sufficiently competent to manage alone?
- Is my knowledge of horse care adequate to ensure the horse's wellbeing?
- If I am buying my child a pony, are they committed to the project?

Do your homework

While many people in the horse world are honest and want to sell the right horse to the right owner, unfortunately there are some unscrupulous ones out there whose primary aim is to make money, regardless of the problems that may ensue. You should always keep this at the front of your mind throughout all your deliberations and make the necessary checks that are outlined in this chapter before you purchase a horse.

Buying the right horse is an exhilarating and rewarding experience. However, acquiring an unsuitable horse – one that may be difficult to handle (even with patient and devoted care) or with an on-going medical condition that means it spends long periods out of work – can be heartbreaking.

You should do everything you can to avoid this situation, which will not only be emotionally draining but could also create financial problems for both you and your family. So make sure you do your homework before you are tempted to buy any horse or pony if you want to enjoy trouble-free ownership. At the very start of your journey to horse ownership, you should consider the questions in the box (left) and try to answer them honestly.

Making time

You may love the idea of owning your own horse but before you rush out and buy one, consider the following issues and think about your answers carefully and realistically:

• How many times a week can you ride? If it's only a couple of times, then perhaps you should consider the possibility of having a sharer (see page 11), or riding at one of the BHS approved riding schools.
• Can you undertake DIY livery yourself? Do you really have enough time to look after your horse on your own without any help?
• Can you take the time off work to attend visits from the farrier, vet and dentist? These professionals will rarely call at weekends or evenings.
• At what level of fitness will you need to keep your horse if you want to compete him at shows? Do you have the time to work him regularly and to maintain that level of fitness?

Riding proficiency

How many of the following activities have you done?
• Riding a horse bareback.
• Jumping a short course of fences of 0.7–0.75 m (2 ft 3 in–2 ft 6 in).
• Hacking out on a cold day.
• Walking, trotting and cantering with no stirrups.
• Getting on a horse that you have never ridden before without feeling worried or apprehensive.
• Riding a friend's horse while they were on holiday.
• Learning to cope with a spook, disobedience or a buck on a horse.
• Riding forward in open countryside.
Someone who has done most of these things would

Cost factors
The costs of owning a horse in the first year could exceed what you pay for him. Keeping a horse at livery anywhere in the UK could cost £3,000–5,000 a year in fees. And that does not include equipment and tack, farrier, veterinary and dentistry bills, show entry fees and travel, if you want to compete. Another major financial outgoing is the cost of regular lessons with a qualified riding teacher.

be considered a *bona fide* novice rider. If several of these things fill you with fear, don't worry, but do put off buying a horse until you have dealt with them. Confide any concerns you might have in your current riding teacher and work towards tackling them. If you are worried about riding an unknown quantity, how are you going to cope with trying out a prospective purchase?

Looking after a horse

If you are considering buying a horse, then your knowledge of horse care should be sufficient to ensure that the horse is looked after properly.

- Do you know the basics of feeding?
- Can you bring in and turn out a sharp horse on a cold day?
- Can you muck out economically and swiftly?

If you are thinking of buying a horse, you must ensure you have adequate time to look after him properly on an everyday basis.

- Can you tack up and untack?
- Do you know how to check whether tack and rugs fit?
- Could you confidently administer first aid to a sick or injured horse until the vet arrives?

These questions are worth thinking about; perhaps before you take the plunge you could work regularly (for free) at a local riding school or livery yard. You will pick up many valuable skills, will probably be offered some free rides (which should complement regular, paid-for lessons) and improve your practical knowledge of horses.

All this would be good preparation for when you have sole charge of your own horse. It will also give you an invaluable insight into what horse ownership entails.

It is also worth considering the halfway house of sharing a horse for a year or so, prior to buying your own. The financial outlay and risks are less serious and it will help you decide if you really want to take the plunge. But remember to draw up a written agreement if you are going to share a horse, to avoid confusion and keep things straightforward.

You can get yourself some valuable experience of stable management by working for free at your local riding school.

The next step

Once you have satisfied yourself that all the key commitment, know-how and financial concerns have been met, you should consider your particular circumstances further.

Will you be keeping the horse at home or at livery? If he is going to be kept at livery, how much will you have to do outside of the agreement? Some livery services do not include hard feed or tack cleaning, and there may be some days that they do not offer certain services. Your stabling and turn-out facilities may have an effect on what type of horse you buy.

Horses for novices

As a novice, you need to find a horse that is suitable for the type of riding you want to do and with the character you are looking for. Don't get bogged down with the breed you prefer; it is more important that the horse is obedient, reactive to your forward aids, feels comfortable to you, and is uncomplicated to care for.

All owners want to have a really rewarding relationship with their horse which can last for years.

The horse's age

This is an important consideration: a novice rider is not the best teacher for a young or inexperienced horse, so you should opt for one that has 'been there and done that' and is in a position to teach you how it's done. You should probably rule out any horse that is younger than seven or eight, and certainly include those from eight up to fourteen or fifteen years.

Nowadays, horses routinely live into their mid-twenties, so it is worthwhile for a novice to consider the fifteen- to twenty-year age range. In this bracket, the likelihood of a veterinary problem is higher, but that may be a risk worth taking for an experienced animal with an illness-free track record behind him.

A horse's age can be assessed approximately by examining the incisor teeth. Don't attempt to do this yourself; ask an experienced person or your vet.

Size

Beware of buying a horse that is not the right size or does not have the suitable weight-carrying ability for you. The horse must not be too big for you — he will look imposing, but not with you dangling from his neck when he starts behaving badly because you are too small to 'keep him together'.

Which breed?

It is misleading to generalize about temperaments and to say which are characteristic of certain breeds. Many riders have happened upon incredibly lazy Thoroughbreds while Cobs can often be quite sharp. Here are a few pointers to help you.

General advice
• All the native breeds are always worth looking at.
• Natives which are crossed with Thoroughbreds are generally adaptable all-rounders – lighter in build than a pure native but able to winter out if necessary.
• Pure Thoroughbreds can make good hacks. Avoid a horse that has been raced professionally, as it may not be ready for a family role.
• Warmbloods have lovely temperaments and can be very rideable. The top dressage and show jumping horses are predominantly Warmbloods, but there are plenty of 'riding horses', bred for non-professionals.

Breed terms
• Cob: A sturdy, weight-carrying horse of no more than 15.3hh.
• Hack: A lightweight horse of Thoroughbred type, usually ranging from 14.2–15.3hh.
• Half-bred: A horse with one parent a Thoroughbred.
• Hotblood or Fullblood: Applies to Eastern breeds, such as Arabs, and to Thoroughbreds.
• Thoroughbred: Horses registered in the General Stud Book which trace their ancestry in the male line back to three Arab stallions.
• Warmblood: Horses with a mixture of blood used for riding and driving.

Connemara ponies are renowned for their versatility and good natures. They are an excellent choice for young riders.

Points of the horse

When people talk about horses and their conformation and anatomy, they will use a wide range of technical terms with which you must familiarize yourself.

Examining a standing horse

The rear end is the engine for movement. It is important that the hindlegs sit well under the body and do not trail behind when the horse is stood up on a hard, flat surface. Viewed from behind, the point of buttock should line up with the centre of the hock and create a straight line through the back of the cannon, fetlock and hoof. In the loin area it is desirable to have a good amount of muscle, making it easy for the horse to connect the momentum from the hind legs over his centre of gravity – giving a nice, balanced ride. The horse's ribs should be nicely rounded and just visible.

The shoulder also plays an important role in the quality of the horse's movement. Ideally, it should slope 45–50 degrees from a horizontal line. This angle should be mirrored in the angle of the pasterns, too. An upright shoulder will normally result in short paces and make it difficult for the horse to lengthen his stride. The top line of the horse stretches from poll to tail and is a good indicator of his fitness. The line should be smooth, and the withers a little higher than the croup. Examine the way the head is set onto the neck. You should be able to fit two fingers into the groove behind the mandible.

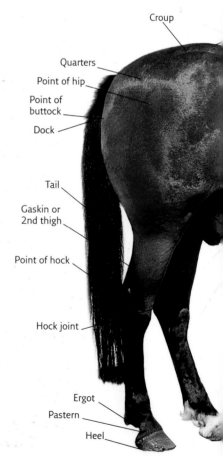

Croup

Quarters

Point of hip

Point of buttock

Dock

Tail

Gaskin or 2nd thigh

Point of hock

Hock joint

Ergot

Pastern

Heel

Examining a moving horse

When a horse is moving, look for a good four-beat walk and a two-beat trot. In the trot, there should be a definite moment of suspension. If the horse over-reaches or forges (you will hear a clanking noise as the hindleg hits a front shoe), he is demonstrating that he is not well balanced – this may be because the pace is too fast.

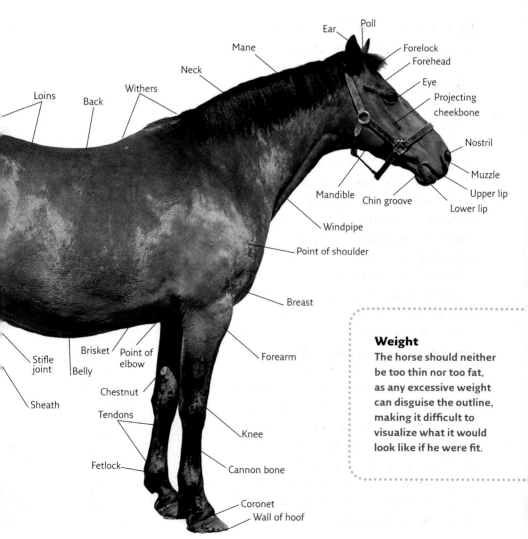

Weight
The horse should neither be too thin nor too fat, as any excessive weight can disguise the outline, making it difficult to visualize what it would look like if he were fit.

Conformation

A trained eye is needed to assess the strengths and weaknesses in a horse's conformation and movement. It is imperative that you take an experienced person with you to viewings.

Watching the movement

Ask to see the horse walked and then trotted in hand. Look for regularity in stride length and the absence of tripping. Watch out for dishing (swinging the front legs to the side as well as to the front in forward movemement) and plaiting (the hind or front legs being put down in each other's path). View the horse from behind and watch if he pushes off with his hind legs to develop forward movement.

Quarters
These should be nicely muscled and not higher than the wither. Watch the relationship between the point of the buttock and back of the cannon, which should be straight when the horse is standing square.

Hocks
The hock is a seat for common problems, often arthritic changes, so watch out for any signs of stiff hindleg action. Capped hocks (normally an enlargement on the point of the hock) are not necessarily a reason to rule out a horse unless you want to show him.

Fetlocks
The fetlock joint should appear flat rather than round. Look for lumps on the front or back, which may be a sign of age. On the inside, they indicate that the horse moves close and brushes. Non-bony lumps called wind galls are only unsightly and rarely cause problems.

Neck
In old-fashioned horseman's tems, the 'neck should be well set-on and the shoulder sloping'. A horse with a low-set neck can be heavy in front to ride. A ewe-neck is to be avoided but is often the result of the horse being ridden in a hollow outline.

Head
This should be in proportion to the horse's size, lean and well set on to the neck so as not to affect respiration or ease of flexion, which can influence the control and balance of the horse.

Back
The horse's back should not be too long; it can prove a weakness for weight carrying if it is, nor should it be dipped in the middle.

Chest
This should be of medium width, not so narrow as to make brushing likely nor so wide as to roll in canter and limit the ability to gallop.

Forelegs
The tendons which run down the backs of legs should be heat-free and without swellings.

Feet
Acquaint yourself with the different types of hoof conformation, ranging from boxy, upright feet to flat feet with low heels.

Where to buy a horse

Before you start looking, think about the horse's height, age, health, character and experience. Breeding and competition record are of secondary importance. A fit, healthy horse, which you can ride effectively and enjoy, is what you need.

Studs

Many studs will buy and sell horses. While they may be their own progeny, they may also do some dealing as part of their establishment. Studs will often sell youngsters that may be backed or ready for backing, but as a novice rider these are not the best sort of horses to start with. If they are selling older, established horses, then take the same precautions as with any dealer.

Advertisements

For the first-time horse owner, look at the ads for horses for sale in the equestrian press and in local horse publications that you can pick up at your tack shop. Advertisers should always offer the following information on any horse or pony that is for sale: its age, height, breeding details, health information and details, such as 'good to shoe', 'box', 'traffic' or 'clip'.

Word of mouth

This can be a good way to find a horse, but exercise extreme caution. Don't rush into buying one that a friend of a friend thinks is perfect for you. It won't do any harm to go and try it, but does it measure up to what you really want? Look at several other horses that are advertised through other media.

Buying a riding school horse or pony for a child can often seem to be a good option, but there may be pitfalls.

Teachers and trainers

Buying through your trainer can be a good way to buy a horse. If you ride at a riding school which has a horse they believe is suitable, it is easy to have a few lessons on the horse and become attached to it, but this can bring problems. It may be very fit and eating lots of hard feed – a lifestyle you will have to change gradually. It may be 'institutionalized' and find life difficult outside of the school. It will be used to living with other horses and may not settle by itself. If your teacher is freelance, then be sure to keep any possible buyer/seller relationship separate from the existing teacher/pupil one.

Dealers

As a novice, how do you distinguish the sharks from the reputable dealers? One of the best ways is word of mouth, but you might not know many people who would have heard about or dealt with a particular dealer. There are various ways to protect yourself. Do you feel comfortable about the dealer's yard and the way they treat the horses? Ask for contact details of previous clients and visit them and their horses. Ask for background on the horse you are interested in and phone up the previous owner to check it out. Consider a trial period (but use a contract) and don't hand over the full price.

Local riding/pony club

Outgrown animals, especially ponies, are often up for sale – this can be an excellent way for you to acquire a safe, reliable pony that knows the ropes. There will also be plenty of third parties who know the animal to ask for information.

Auctions

Take an experienced horse owner with you. Look at the vetting papers thoroughly and be clear about different types of vet certificate. Try the horse before you buy and see how it reacts. Establish a rapport with the seller and tell them about yourself to give them an opportunity to be honest about the horse's health and character.

Going to see a horse

Once you have some horses in mind, whether they are sourced from advertisements or word of mouth, speak to the sellers. Plan out how you are going to describe yourself, your riding ability and the sort of home you are offering the horse.

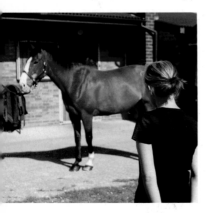

When you go to view a horse, do take a good look at him. Make sure that you observe his behaviour as well as his conformation and watch him in action, too.

Preparing for the visit

Discuss how best to describe your riding ability with your riding teacher. It is vital that you are as open and honest as possible, otherwise you could waste valuable time and money visiting an unsuitable horse, while a much better match for you is sold to someone else. If you are a first-time horse owner, have ridden for less than a year, or are nervous, you really should tell the seller in advance of a visit. They will then be able to help you to make a decision as to whether it is worth your visiting the horse.

Wasting time

You will often see the words 're-advertised due to timewasters' featured in advertisements; while this may not be the case, horse owners do get fed up with putting time aside for a prospective purchaser who has misrepresented themselves.

Of course, this can work in the opposite way, too, but it is just a part of buying. It is always worth riding a horse if you think that it might be suitable, but do not get on any horse that is displaying signs of dangerous behaviour. The person selling the horse should always ride the horse with you watching before you get on and also offer a brief description of what he is like to ride.

Questions you should ask

Basic questions
- How old is the horse?
- What breed is it?
- What types of work does it do?
- Has it had competition success?
- How long has the current owner had it and do they know about any previous owners?

Veterinary questions
- Has the horse ever received veterinary treatment for lameness?
- What was the condition?
- What was the treatment?
- Has the horse ever had colic?
- How serious was it?
- Has the horse had laminitis?
- Has it had any other illness which has meant the vet has been called?
- Has it ever had an accident?
- What was the treatment and how long was the recovery period?
- Has the owner ever made a claim on the horse's insurance?

Temperament questions
- Does the horse enjoy company: of people and other horses?
- Is it ever aggressive to people?
- Is it ever aggressive to horses?
- Is it good in traffic?
- Does the horse hack out alone and in company without problems?
- Does it get strong when cantered on open ground?
- Does the horse enjoy shows?
- When stressed, how does the horse's behaviour change?
- Does the horse load easily?
- Has it ever cribbed, wind-sucked or weaved? If so, when?
- Is it happy to stand tied up?

Current rider questions
- What level is the current rider?
- Do they compete the horse?
- Do they carry a whip?
- Who trains the horse and rider?
- Can you speak to the trainer?

Stable management questions
- Is the horse turned out or stabled?
- What type of forage does it eat?
- What type of hard feed does it eat?
- Is it stabled in a barn or in boxes?
- Is the horse good to clip?
- Is the horse good to shoe?

The day of the visit

As the prospective owner, you must attend all the viewings in person, preferably with an experienced horse person. Confirm that you are keeping the appointment made and make sure that you arrive on time, dressed suitably in riding gear.

The owner should allow you to examine the horse closely before walking and trotting it up for you and then riding it.

Checking the horse

Keep your eyes open. As you arrive, monitor the conditions on the yard, from the point of view of how the horses kept there are being stabled and also the behaviour of the other horses and any people on the yard. Be businesslike, not over-friendly or excited. The person who is selling the horse should present the horse groomed but untacked. Spend some time in the stable with the horse, for a preliminary look over it, and then ask the owner your most important questions (see page 21).

Once you are satisfied that all is well, the owner should tack the horse up with you present and proceed to ride it for you. This will take some time, as all horses should be properly warmed up before being put through their paces. You must observe everything carefully. The horse should be shown to you doing all the things that you will wish to do with it, such as jumping a small round of fences. If everything seems satisfactory, you should ride next, not the experienced person you've brought along to advise, or the trainer.

Relax and take your time; ask the current owner as many questions as you like and remember 'safety first'. Again, if the horse is being bought because you want to jump with him, make sure you take him over

at least one fence. If at any time you feel unsafe or out of your depth, then bring the session to an end.

If everything seems in order, you could ask if your experienced friend or trainer could try out the horse. But remember that the horse has already done a lot of work so it might be best to arrange a second visit. In addition, you may want to walk the horse round a field or down a nearby road or bridlepath, if he looks promising. But, again, don't expect this on a first visit.

A second visit for a good prospect can be arranged whereby you set the agenda – perhaps taking him for a short hack or onto the road, but get the owner's agreement beforehand. Never take a seller's word for it that a horse can do something, unless you have ridden the horse yourself in those particular circumstances.

Ask the vendor to trot the horse up for you and then watch the movements carefully from every angle: from the side, the front and from behind. Look out for any tell-tale signs of lameness or poor conformation.

Pitfalls at a viewing

Observation and questions are your best friends at a viewing. While the majority of vendors will be genuine, some are not. Look for possible signs that

Always ride the horse before making a decision. Taking it on a trial basis is the best option.

When trying out the horse, put it through its paces and practise some trotting and cantering.

the horse was ridden before you came – sweat marks where tack has been, and unease when seeing the tack arrive for your trial.

Check that the horse has adequate forage and water – this is one way of quietening a normally boisterous horse. At the other extreme, some people may even use sedatives to calm a horse, so look out for any inflammation of the soft tissue around the horse's eyes, a relaxed sheath in a gelding, and tripping. Don't ride a horse which you think may be doped; just make your excuses and leave.

If you intend to or have to hack on roads, then it is important that you try the horse in traffic. Do not just take the vendor's word for it that the horse is good in these situations.

Further checks

If the horse is being sold with a competition record or perhaps points from one of the competitive disciplines, then check this out with the appropriate sport organization. To check the horse's registration with the breed societies, ask to see the papers and also take down the number, if the vendor has one.

A simple internet search will often bring up the contact details for the many breed associations and showing societies with whom you can make contact. They are always happy to help you with advice and checking things out if you explain the situation in full.

You must go back and visit the horse more than once, increasing the level of detail and involvement each time. If the horse and the vendor are going to a show, then go along and watch them in action. You cannot have too much information about your prospective purchase. Don't rush into making a decision about the first horse you see; there is more than just one suitable horse out there for you and you owe it to yourself and your horse to look around to make sure that you find the right one.

Trial periods

Find out whether you can have the horse on a trial basis and draw up a contract outlining the terms on both sides, which may include a deposit changing hands. Most owners will not allow their horses to go out on trial and this is for good reason: in the wrong hands, a horse can be spoilt quickly and will then be returned as unwanted. The owner is left without a proper sale and with a horse that needs to be rehabilitated, necessitating even more money and time to be spent on the horse.

If the owner will not allow you to take the horse on a trial basis, do make sure that you visit again and take him out for another ride in order to get the feel of him before deciding to buy.

Five-stage vetting

Once you have settled on a horse and can tick all the boxes, then you are ready to make a purchase. However, you should always get a five-stage vetting for a horse or pony first.

The vet will want to observe the movement of the horse as he is walked, trotted up and turned.

Reasons for vetting

• It will make it easier to get good value insurance for the horse (saving you money in the long term).
• Although you have done all your checks, the vet is in a much better position to judge a horse's health.
• The vet can judge the horse's temperament, behaviour and its suitability for you.

Practical steps

The five-stage vetting should be carried out by a vet who is a horse specialist and is known to you. Do not use the vendor's vet. If you don't know an equine vet in the area where your horse lives, use the internet site www.findavet.org.uk. Give the veterinary clinic not only the address of the yard but also details of the horse (so the wrong one is not vetted) and the facilities (hard trot-up areas, surfaced arenas, etc.).

Decide whether you want a blood test taken, just in case a problem arises and you suspect the owner may have administered painkillers or even dope.

Buyer's report

The vet will produce a document detailing all their findings, i.e. signs of disease or injury, and will offer a judgment on the suitability of the horse for the job intended. They will often give a verbal run-through of this immediately, which can help you make a decision.

The stages of the vetting

Stage 1

A preliminary examination is made of the whole horse. This monitors the heart at rest, eyesight, mouth and teeth. Examination of the teeth will give the vet an approximate idea of the age of the horse as well as any problems that may make acceptance of the bit or eating difficult. The horse will be examined all over by hand (palpated), and the vet will check the horse's back and foot conformation and balance.

Stage 2

The vet will then trot up the horse on a hard surface for around 20–30 m. The horse will be backed up and turned sharply both ways, after which flexion tests will be performed and the horse trotted again. The flexion tests may highlight problems in movement brought about by arthritic conditions and other things, such as neurological diseases like shivers.

Stage 3

The horse is saddled up and the vet will monitor its reaction prior to a period of strenuous work. The aim is to monitor heart and lung health. The amount of exercise will vary according to the horse's fitness and age. In ridden exercise, the horse's gait and response to the rider can be checked. The heart will be monitored again once the exercise is over and tack removed.

Stage 4

While the horse recovers in the stable, the vet will monitor its health during recovery from strenuous exercise. The vet may also look over the horse again and palpate parts of its body.

Stage 5

The horse's feet will be inspected and then the horse will be trotted again. This is to discover if it has any post-exercise stiffness.

Legal aspects

Your legal position will vary, depending on whether you have purchased your horse or pony from a private individual or from a business, such as a dealer or at an auction.

You must never rush into buying a horse. Once you have brought him home, it is difficult to send him back again.

Private individuals

Here the adage 'let the buyer beware' stands. You have no rights other than the description of the horse as it appears in the advertisement. It can, however, be useful to ask the vendor to send a document outlining the main aspects of the horse, i.e. the age, breeding, experience, height, lack of vices, behaviour when clipped, loaded, on roads, with the farrier, etc.

Dealers

If you buy a horse from a dealer, there is a piece of law known as the Sale of Goods Act 1979 (intended for miscellaneous second-hand goods) that protects the buyer in certain ways. The three main points of this are that the horse:

● Must be fit and healthy as it is described.

● Must be suitable for the purpose sold, i.e. for a novice rider who is a first-time horse owner.

● Must be as described by the vendor; this covers the basics, such as the horse's height, colour, breeding, etc.

Nevertheless, it is still up to you, the purchaser, to check out particular details, including health and behaviour, e.g. when loading, as well as the horse's history – has he ever been used in a riding school, for example?

Auctions

Auctions will have their own terms and conditions which are set out in their catalogues. Horses that are sold with a warranty will have a specified date by which they must be returned, i.e. seven days. However, if you buy a horse unwarranted, then you will have no recourse if the horse turns out not to be suitable.

Horse passports

On February 28 2005, it became law for all horses to be sold with a passport, so make sure your purchase has one. You need to contact the passport issuing office, which could be the BHS or a breed society – it will be clear on the passport – and notify them of your name, address and the horse's identification number. This must be done within 30 days of the change of ownership.

The cost of horse ownership

Apart from the initial cost of purchase, keeping a horse is a continual financial commitment. Unless it comes with its own tack, you will need a properly fitting saddle, bridle, girths, a head collar and lead rope, grooming equipment, first-aid kit, stable and turn-out rugs, yard and feeding equipment. All tack and rugs should be correctly fitted by a qualified person, whether new or second-hand. You will also need sensible, comfortable clothing, protective headgear, boots and gloves. Safety gear is essential and should never be skimped on. Don't be tempted to save money buying a second-hand hat that could have been damaged previously. Then there is the cost of keeping your horse, whether it's on your own land, in a rented paddock, in a stable or at livery. The horse needs bedding, feed and forage, as well as regular visits from the farrier. These are the basic costs of ownership. Additional considerations are the cost of dental, veterinary and routine health care, including worming and vaccinations. You can take out insurance from an equine insurance broker to cover veterinary fees. If you are a novice or a more experienced rider, you will benefit from instruction. Regular lessons will help you to become a better and a safer rider. And if you plan to compete with your horse, there will be additional equipment, tack and clothing, as well as entry fees to shows and competitions, not to mention a horsebox or trailer for transporting your horse.

Settling in your horse

The golden rule when you are settling in your new horse is to make things as similar to his old home as possible and only to introduce your own changes to his diet and routine gradually.

It is extremely important that you establish a good relationship with your new horse. He will soon look forward to your visits to feed, water or exercise him.

Make your horse at home

Within your capabilities, initially, you should keep the horse to the same stabling and turn-out arrangement as he had before you bought him. Try to obtain a few days' supply of his old forage and hard feed and only introduce any dietary changes gradually.

Always resist the temptation to shower the new arrival with carrots, apples, new rugs, gawping strangers, etc. However, do ride him for a short time, once he has had a few hours to settle in, or, at the latest, on the following day, especially if he is fit and accustomed to regular exercise.

You should not leave it for too long before setting up your next appointment with the farrier as the horse will be new on the list and you will need to give the farrier time to book him in to his diary. Set up any other appointments that you may feel you need, such as, say, a fitting with a master saddler for a new saddle or getting the horse's current saddle checked out.

Problem-busting

If there is a problem with your new horse, you must talk to the previous owner about it. Be calm and tactful and see if they can offer a sensible solution or might have experienced the same problem in the past. Always aim to solve problems amicably, but if you think there is a serious mismatch or the horse has been misrepresented in some way, you should do everything you can to get the owner to take the horse back – you may lose money but it will still make sense in the long run.

If you have bought the horse from someone in the trade, such as a horse dealer, then you should always set out the problem in writing, tell them what you would like done and give them a date by which to reply. You can take a problem with a dealer to the local trading standards officer.

The first few weeks

During the initial stage, the horse will be adjusting and settling in to his new home environment. You can spend this time enjoying his company as you get to know each other. Make a point of spending time with your horse, looking after and feeding him yourself, and exercising him every day if possible.

Check with the previous owner when the horse was last wormed and ask your vet to perform a faecal egg count to make sure your newcomer does not have a high worm burden and will not infect the pasture on which he will graze. Arrange for a visit from the farrier to ensure the horse does not have to wait longer than four to six weeks from his last shoeing. Your vet can inspect his teeth for any signs of abnormal wear and other dental problems. If you already own other horses, introduce him to them gradually in order to avoid bullying and to allow changes in the established pecking order. Putting him in an adjoining field initially is a good option if this is possible. It is also sensible to take some riding lessons with your new horse and use this as an opportunity to improve your riding skills. There is always room for improvement.

want to know more?
• Look at the selection of horses for sale in the equestrian press
• To find out more about qualified instructors, contact the BHS
• Check out insurance companies specializing in equine insurance; BHS members receive automatic public liability cover
• For horse passports, contact the passport issuing office, e.g. BHS or breed societies

weblinks
• Visit the BHS website at: www.bhs.org.uk
• Visit the British Veterinary Association website at: www.bva.co.uk
• Visit Horse and Hound magazine's website at: www.horseandhound.co.uk

2 Stabling your horse

A good way to keep a horse healthy and happy is to turn him out daily in a well-managed field. However, even when he can live out most of the time, there will be occasions when he needs suitable housing. Some people believe routine stabling is undesirable and all horses should be turned out day and night, but this is often impractical. Even when it is possible and appropriate, adequate shelter must be provided. A good regime for most horses and owners is to turn them out during the day and stable them at night, or vice versa, varying the turn-out periods according to the weather and grazing.

Stable systems

Most people keep their horses at livery, where facilities are rented and, depending on whether you opt for a DIY, assisted- or full-livery system, help may be provided. In assessing livery yards, stabling must be looked at as part of the overall package, but the same guidelines apply when you are building accommodation.

Planning

Find out whether you will need planning permission for a stable at home, whether building it from scratch or adapting existing buildings. It is easier to get permission for timber stables than permanent brick ones. Talk to neighbours and allay any fears about noise and smell. Think the project through down to the fine detail of where to site a muck heap and how you will dispose of manure.

Suitable stables

If you can keep your horse at home and put up new stables or convert existing buildings, you can create an ideal environment. However, you may want to start off at livery with the support of a knowledgeable yard owner. Before taking the plunge and going it alone at home, examine your lifestyle and the time you have available for looking after a horse. You will also need to consider whether your facilities are suitable: do you have a stable and a paddock and a properly fenced field for turning out and grazing? Do you have a friend or family member who can help out? Every horse owner needs a back-up system for times when they are busy or away on holiday. Before you buy a horse, answer the following questions.
• If this is your first horse, do you have someone knowledgeable to whom you can turn for advice?
• Do you have access to a safe area to school in?

Even if you are not interested in competing, you and your horse will benefit from schooling sessions and lessons to keep you both interested and up to scratch. This includes riders who concentrate on hacking, as an obedient, responsive horse is a much greater pleasure to hack and is safer.

Most horses enjoy company, whether it is just looking out over the stable door or grazing together outside in a paddock.

Down to basics

The foundations of the stables are as important as the building itself. Today, concrete is the standard flooring because it is easy to keep clean. However, it is very important that it is prepared to the correct specifications. Laying concrete is a specialist job, and to aid drainage (to drains set outside rather than inside the box) the floor must be laid with a slight fall, or slope, to the rear of the box so that any urine runs out to external drains rather than pooling on the floor. For most people, the best option will be to employ a specialist building contractor to do this job rather than attempt it themselves or to use someone with no experience of laying a stable floor.

Stable specifications

There are two main stabling systems: external looseboxes and internal stabling, which is constructed within an existing or purpose-built building. The indoor system is often called the American barn system as it was first popular in the United States.

Doors should be the correct height to enable the horse to look over the top and observe what is going on outside in the yard.

Which system?

Each system has its pros and cons. External stables are cheaper to build, but unless careful thought goes into their design, horses can seem isolated from their neighbours. Internal stables are more pleasant for the owner looking after the horses because they are under cover, but they are harder to ventilate and can lead to bullying between horses. In most cases, they are only feasible if you want to provide housing for at least four horses.

Size and cost

Individual stables, whether internal or external, should always be as large as possible. The minimum recommendations are usually 3.04 m (10 ft) square for a pony up to about 14.2 hands; 3.65 m (12 ft) square for a horse up to about 16 hands; and 4.26 m (14 ft) square for a horse of 16.2 hands and over.

It is important to recognize, however, that these are the minimum recommendations and that all horses and ponies will appreciate having as much space as possible. Larger stables are also more economical in terms of bedding, as although you need to put down more to start with, they are usually easier to keep clean because any droppings are less likely to be kicked around.

Although we all have to work to a budget, it is more economical in the long run to look ahead and build for future as well as present needs. Thus, most manufacturers charge relatively less per unit for putting up, say, three stables and a hay store than for building just two stables. You will also find that you can never have too much storage space.

Outside looseboxes which are made of wood may need to be treated with a wood preservative to protect them and keep them in good order.

Linings and doors

Go for the best specifications that you can afford. Linings (also known as kickboards, for obvious reasons) to full height are more expensive than ones that go halfway up the wall, but they improve insulation as well as minimizing any damage to the stable framework from flying hooves.

Door openings should be at least 1.22 m (4 ft) wide to prevent a horse banging its hips as it goes in and out, and internal headroom should be a minimum of 3.65 m (12 ft) and preferably 3.8 m (12 ft 6 in).

Air vents high up in the outside back walls of looseboxes will provide better air circulation.

Stable roofs should be pitched rather than flat with an overhang to keep both you and the horse dry in wet weather.

In theory, this could be reduced for a small pony, but in practice, the greater the headroom, the greater the volume of air, which helps with ventilation.

Conventional hinged doors should always open outwards, so if a horse got cast (stuck while trying to roll) against the door it would be possible to open it. They must also have a sliding bolt at the top and a kickover latch at the bottom for security – some horses are accomplished escape artists. A galvanized metal anti-chew strip fitted to the top edge of the bottom door should help to prevent any damage from chewing by the horse.

Good ventilation

This is essential for the health of your horse's respiratory system, which is why it is important to keep the top half of your stable door open even in bad weather. If you are worried that your horse will get cold, add an extra or a different rug. Avoid

draughts which can give a horse a chill. Air vents should be at different heights to maximize the airflow. The general recommendation for outdoor stabling is that inlets should be just above horse height and outlets should be in the roof ridge, giving maximum air circulation. The air is warmed by the horse, then rises and goes out through the roof. For internal stabling, get specialist advice.

The roof

Whether you opt for external looseboxes or internal stabling, the roof should be pitched rather than flat, to provide the maximum volume of air inside the stable. Several materials are used for outdoor stables but corrugated cement sheets or Onduline sheeting are both popular. Inserting a translucent perspex roof panel will let in more light.

An overhang on the roof over the door and front wall area of outside looseboxes is well worth having, as it gives extra shelter in bad weather for both the horse and the groom. In the case of prefabricated stabling, the overhang is usually an extension of the roof, but with brick or block stabling, it can be a continuation of the roof or even a separate material. Guttering is usually standard along the front of the stable and, again, it is often worth investing in some extra guttering at the back.

Drainage systems

Your stable will need some sort of drainage system, and you may need to get professional advice on which is the best one to use. Looseboxes and barns should have a shallow slope of one in sixty towards the front or the back of the box.

An overhang extension of the roof over the stable door and front wall area will help protect you and your horse from bad weather and provide shade.

Always ensure that stable doors are closed and securely bolted. Many horses and ponies are skilled at opening them.

Any liquid can be directed through a small opening in the centre of the wall at floor level into an open drain running along the outside of the stable wall. You can install removable traps to collect any straw and solids which might otherwise block the drains.

Floors

These should be constructed in such a way that they provide comfort for the horse and not put strain on its legs. The optimum floor space for a horse should be 11–14 sq m (118–150 sq ft). The most commonly used material is concrete. Easy to put down, it must be laid at a minimum depth of 15 cm (6 in) over a well-drained base of hard core and shingle. You must also install a damp course. The mix must be extra hard to withstand the horse's weight and urine, and the surface should be roughened to make it nonslip.

Alternative materials include: chalk and clay which are cheap but require more maintenance and are rarely used these days; composition flooring which is good but very expensive; porous floors which need a well-drained base and can be smelly; and rubber matting placed over the top of concrete, which saves time mucking out. Rubber matting should be used with some form of absorbent bedding, such as shavings or hemp, to absorb urine and help keep rugs as clean as possible. Matting gives a warmer floor when the horse lies down, avoids the risk of capped hocks and elbows, and may allow you to use less bedding than on a concrete floor.

Electricity

Any electrical systems and wiring in a stable should be installed by a qualified electrician – even a low voltage can kill a horse. You will need a trip switch system with cabling running through unchewable metal pipes, and any switches positioned outside the box out of the horse's reach. You can install fluorescent lights or bulb fixtures high in the roof of the box, or bulkhead light fittings at a more accessible height for replacing and cleaning the light bulbs. All bulbs should have transparent covers.

Maintenance

The stable buildings, equipment and fittings will need regular maintenance to keep them in good condition and prevent deterioration. Woodwork will need to be treated with preservatives to ensure that it stays weatherproof and looks smart, as will any wooden doors and windows. Alternatively, you may choose to paint them but do not use toxic lead-based paints. Metal doors and windows made of rust-proof, galvanized iron or steel will not need any attention but their hinges might.

Other stable buildings

In addition to the looseboxes, it is a good idea if you have room to have a specially constructed feed shed, which is built of bricks or concrete blocks in order to discourage rats and other vermin.

You will also need a tack room which can be securely locked. Tack is a security risk and attractive to burglars; check with your insurance company before installing one. If you have the space and the budget, put in a sink with hot and cold water to make cleaning tack easier. Although you will need lighting, heating is not essential as there is must be no direct heat to leather saddles and bridles.

A watering system is useful for providing fresh, clean water for filling water troughs and buckets.

Optional fittings
Grids and grilles may be fixed to the top door of looseboxes. V-shaped grids are sometimes used to stop weaving, but they do not prevent the cause. They enable the horse to put his head and neck over the door, but the opening must be large enough for him to draw back without hitting his head.

Fixtures and fittings

Not everyone has the luxury of electricity in their stables, but it makes a huge difference. Installing it is a specialist job for a qualified electrician, and it is important to make sure that everything to do with it is horse-, water- and vermin-proof.

Wood shavings can make a warm and comfortable bed for a horse. Many are dust extracted.

Feeding

There are several different ways of delivering your horse's food. Feeding from ground level is the most natural way but it is not always practical because food and forage get mixed up in bedding. Haynets should always be set at eyelevel; if positioned too high, your horse will be stretching his neck at an unnatural angle to feed, and there will also be a risk that some of the hay seeds will fall into his eyes.

Hard feed is best provided in a feed bowl on the stable floor; this can be removed when the horse has finished eating. Some people use feed bowls that clip over the door, but this is an unnatural position for the horse. Permanent mangers in boxes should be avoided as they are a potential hazard.

Watering

Water must always be available. Automatic water suppliers do have obvious benefits but you cannot monitor how much your horse is actually drinking. Buckets of water placed on the floor can be kicked over but are easily cleaned. Special bucket holders fixed to the wall can be used in cases where a horse is prone to knocking over buckets. Alternatively, an old tyre can often make a firm base for a water bucket to help prevent this happening.

Bedding

Many types of bedding are available, ranging from traditional wheat straw to dried wood fibre and even elephant grass. An important consideration is whether the bedding you choose will help minimize the dust and spores in your horse's stable; in some cases, this may mean that wheat straw is unsuitable. You also need to consider cost, ease of handling and disposal, availability and storage considerations.

It is important that whatever type of bedding you choose, it encourages your horse to lie down and rest in comfort without any risk of injuring himself. It should also keep him warm and minimize draughts. It should create a nonslip surface on the floor of the loosebox or stall, so that the horse cannot slip when he is moving around the stable. This will also help to reduce any jar to his legs when he is moving around or standing still on the hard floor.

Some bedding materials, e.g. paper, can be heavy to handle when wet, and do not rot down easily. Other types vary in quality: wood shavings from one manufacturer may be significantly more dusty than those from another, even though both sorts could be marketed as dust-extracted bedding. Never use materials sourced directly from the building trade and which have not been screened, as they may contain nails and other potential hazards.

Straw

This is widely used as bedding, as the manure can be easily disposed of; it looks inviting and clean; and it is relatively cheap to purchase in years of good harvests. However, if it is eaten by the horse, it may cause allergies and coughing.

Equipment

Only basic equipment should be fitted inside your horse's stable. This will usually comprise the following items:
- A ring for tying up your horse when necessary
- A water trough or bucket
- A haynet and tie ring (optional)

Although shavings will make a comfortable spore-free bed for a horse, the manure can be quite difficult to dispose of.

Wheat straw is preferable to barley or oat straw, but it is not always readily available. It must be good quality, and the horse must be discouraged from eating it as this can make him overweight and affect his fitness. Spraying non-toxic disinfectant on the bedding can help prevent this. Another problem with using straw as bedding is that it creates dust and can act as a host to fungal spores. When these are inhaled, they can lead to allergic coughing.

The system of deep litter bedding, where the bottom layer is left undisturbed for several weeks and fresh bedding put on top, is not recommended as the build-up of ammonia from compacted urine and droppings is a severe threat to a horse's respiratory system. It is even more of a hazard if the stable has poor drainage. Deep litter bedding also generates heat and this, together with ammonia, predisposes the horse's feet to fungal infections.

Shavings and sawdust

Compressed baled shavings are less dusty than sawdust, but both provide spore-free bedding. The other advantage is that the horse will not eat them, unlike straw. Packed in polythene bags, baled shavings are easy to store and they are relatively free of dust.

Shredded paper

Shredded paper or cardboard, which can be bought in wrapped bales, can be useful for horses with respiratory problems linked to dust or mould spores. Disposal can be a problem, and in some areas it may have to be disposed of by a professional contractor. It can take longer to break down than some types of bedding and is particularly untidy in windy conditions.

Rubber matting

This is a popular choice, but unless it is sealed to the floor so that no liquid can seep underneath it only works well in combination with excellent drainage and scrupulous management. Rubber matting with a topping of highly absorbent bedding material is generally effective, and the matting will add warmth and a cushioning effect to a concrete floor.

Other bedding

New bedding materials are being developed all the time, including some made from wood fibre, flax straw and elephant grass. Hemp is another common material, but take care that the horse does not eat it. If this happens, use another form of bedding.

Straw makes a warm bed, but it should be mucked out on a daily basis with the horse taken out of the stable while you do so.

Disposing of manure

When choosing bedding, consider how you are going to manage and dispose of the manure. Some materials are claimed to reduce the size of manure heaps to the extent that they can be disposed of easily. To get rid of large heaps you may have to pay a professional contractor, and the cost will rise if you use a bedding material that does not rot down quickly.

Building a muck heap

A muck heap should be sited within easy reach of the stables. Ideally, it should have a concrete base with one side open and the other sides built up to a height of 1.8 m (6 ft) – use railway sleepers or concrete blocks. It will need daily care, and the manure should be built in steps with a flat top to allow it to absorb rain and rot down. Keep the sides vertical and well raked down, and the surrounding area clean.

Damping down
This practice is not recommended, so any bedding that is sufficiently dusty to need damping down is unsuitable for your horse. Damp bedding does not provide a good environment and it encourages the growth of mould spores.

Bedding down

Bedding should be deep enough that when a fork is stuck into it, the prongs do not touch the floor. Banks of bedding round the sides of the stable will keep out draughts, prevent abrasions if a horse is lying down against a wall, and stop it becoming wedged if it is lying down and then unable to rise (cast).

1 Using a fork, pile the straw up against a wall. Once a week, disinfect the floor and leave it to air and dry for an hour or two before replacing the bedding.

Healthy, contented horses

Some horses love to eat straw bedding while others are allergic to fungal spores in the straw which can cause coughing. For them, wood shavings, chopped hemp, dust-extracted straw or shredded paper are better materials, although these are more expensive than straw. To keep your horse healthy and happy, it is worth paying the extra for the right bedding.

2 When the floor is completely dry, bring the old straw back into the middle of the box and then spread it over the floor. Use the new bedding to make banks round the walls of the stable.

3 Bank the bedding up against the walls of the stable, making it a little deeper around the sides. To test whether the bed is deep enough, turn the fork upside down and push onto the straw – you should not feel the floor.

Mucking out

Mucking out the stable is an essential daily job. An important form of basic hygiene, it helps minimize the risk of poor health and ailments and will keep the horse's living quarters dry and comfortable. Make it part of your everyday routine – when it is done correctly, using the right equipment, it need not take long.

1 Start by shovelling out any visible droppings and then transporting them away to the muck heap, which should be sited away from the stable but within easy reach.

Equipment

For mucking out your horse or pony, you will need to get the following items of equipment: a wheelbarrow, a shovel or long-handled scoop, a yard brush and a stable fork. It is essential that you turn the horse out of the stable, and also that you remove any buckets or portable water containers while you are mucking out your horse's loosebox.

2 Separate the wet bedding from the dry with a two-prong fork. Throw the dry straw to one side; put the wet bedding into a wheelbarrow.

3 Finally, sweep the stable floor with a sturdy brush and then replace the straw, taking extra from one of the banks around the walls.

Horse-friendly housing

Horses are sociable animals and more relaxed if they can see their neighbours. The top half of a dividing wall between their stables should comprise a metal grille, which will help with air circulation and light. However, it does mean that neighbouring horses always need to be compatible and healthy.

Other remedies
All stabled horses should have hay or haylage to mimic their natural grazing behaviour, especially if they show stereotypic behaviour. Stable toys may also help keep some stabled horses happier. The most successful toys can be pushed around the floor, releasing a small amount of hidden feed and mimicking the horse's natural foraging behaviour. Don't use them as a substitute for turning out and/or exercising your horse.

Stable vices

Some horses dislike being confined in a stable. This can result in unwanted behaviour once known as 'stable vices' but now referred to as stereotypic behaviour. The three most common are: weaving, crib-biting and wind-sucking.

A horse that weaves swings its head from side to side, usually over the stable door. It may shift from one front foot to the other, putting strain on its limbs. Crib-biters grab hold of a convenient surface, usually the top of the door or a window ledge, and hold on to it, taking in air at the same time, while windsuckers take in air without holding on.

The best remedy is to turn out the affected horse as much as possible, and if it has to be stabled to make the environment as horse-friendly as possible. This is where a barn set-up can help. Anti-weaving grilles are V-shaped metal frames that fit on top of the stable door and limit the side to side movement of the horse's head. They may prevent the behaviour in some cases but will probably not reduce the stress that causes it. Some horses will simply weave behind the grille. Painting an unpleasant-tasting substance on the stable door may help to deter a horse from crib-biting, but will not take away the need to do so.

Storage space

As well as stabling for your horse, you will also need some space to store his feed, clean bedding, hay or haylage, rugs and tack.

Storing feed

This must be kept under cover and stored in vermin-proof containers. Purpose-built feed bins, filled from the top and then emptied from the bottom, are ideal. Metal dustbins with securely fitting lids are cheaper and more serviceable. If you store bagged feed in a dustbin, leave it in the bag so you don't keep putting new feed on top of old.

Storing hay

A weatherproof building with good ventilation is best. Hay stores should be sited far enough away from stables to prevent dust and spores contaminating your horse's living space. Some American barn designs include overhead lofts, but these are an environmental and a fire risk. Wrapped and bagged haylage can be stored outside the stable.

Bridles should be hung up in order to keep the top rounded.

Storing tack

Tack theft has become a problem and the safest option is to store your saddle and bridle in the house where it cannot be seen from outside. Individual tack storage units which look like large metal safes and bolt to the floor are another option, as are locking saddle racks. Whatever type of building your tack is stored in, it should be kept dry, as damp conditions will encourage the growth of mould. Tack should not be stored directly over a heat source, e.g. a radiator.

Storing rugs
Clean rugs can be stored in trunks, while storage racks installed under cover are ideal for rugs that are in use. Heated storage racks will dry off the outdoor rugs more quickly.

Daily routine

A horse is not usually kept in its stable night and day, unless the weather is bad, the animal is unwell, or there are other pressing reasons for stabling it temporarily. Horses need plenty of space to exercise and stretch their legs, roll around when they feel inclined and generally enjoy themselves outside in the open air.

If your horse is stabled, you must provide feed and forage for him each day as well as fresh water.

Turning out your horse

A horse housed indoors permanently can become irritable and prone to stable vices, leg swelling and digestive upsets. Stabling your horse at night and turning him out during the day is a good routine to get into. At the very least, a stable-kept horse should always have four hours outside, either being ridden or wandering in pasture, so that he can graze and exercise. In summer, you may have to use a fly fringe to keep worrisome flies away from his eyes, whereas in winter he may need to wear an outdoor rug for warmth, especially if his coat has been clipped.

Time dedication

Even if your horse lives outside all the year round, you need to check on him every day and provide food and fresh water. You may also have to check his rugs, exercise and groom him, and pick out his feet. If he is stabled, he will need regular mucking out. Owning a horse is time-consuming and you need to devote time to caring for him and adapt your daily routine in order to do so. A healthy horse needs routine, which means that you will have to feed him at the same time each day, as changes to his usual regime may upset him and may even predispose him to colic.

At livery

If you do not have room for a stable nor own a paddock, you may decide to keep your horse at livery. This means that you rent the facilities for looking after him. There are different systems, including full livery, do-it-yourself livery and working livery.

Choosing a livery yard

Look at the stabling and grazing facilities, general cleanliness, health and demeanour of the horses, the friendliness of the staff and whether it is a working livery where your horse could be used for lessons or ridden out. It is vital that your horse is healthy and happy and has a regular feeding and exercise routine.

Full livery

The horse is fed, groomed and even exercised for you by the livery staff. Thus your horse is well looked after and your duties are limited – ideal for busy people who do not have the time or facilities to care for a horse themselves nor to ride regularly. The downside is that it is an extremely expensive arrangement.

Working livery

You agree a system that works for both of you with a riding school, with clearly defined areas regarding responsibility and who pays for what.

Do-it-yourself livery

Livery is much cheaper if you do the grooming, tack cleaning, mucking out and exercising the horse yourself. Clearly define the conditions in advance and agree them in writing, signed by both parties.

want to know more?
- For stables at home, check with your local planning authority
- Get your stables and yard assessed by the local fire prevention and crime prevention officers for safety
- Check out the livery yards in your area and what services they offer
- Ask your vet and local saddlers shops about dust-free bedding
- See the BHS leaflet on bedding for horses

weblinks
- Visit the BHS website at: www.bhs.org.uk
- For the BHS National Livery Plan launched to find good livery yards, visit the website at: www.horsedata.co.uk

3 Grass management

If your horse could choose whether he lived in a stable or out at grass, he would certainly opt for a life at grass. Roaming about and grazing are what a horse is designed to do. Compared with keeping him in a stable it might also seem the easier option for you, the owner – generally it is. Nevertheless, there is far more to keeping your horse at grass than simply turning him loose in a field and shutting the gate. You will have to manage the land, provide shelter against heat, cold, wind and rain, and maintain fencing and gates in a good state of repair.

Pasture care

In their wild state, horses are free to wander far and wide in their search for food. Nowadays, horses are kept in very confined conditions, and nothing will turn land into a dust-bowl or a quagmire more quickly than over-grazing by our equine friends.

Whether your horse is kept at grass or turned out to graze each day for a few hours, you will need some well-managed pasture.

Getting started

For the good of your horse and your land, find out how to manage what grazing land you have in the most efficient way. Horses are selective grazers, and you can recognize a badly managed field by bare patches, where the occupants have grazed the palatable plants right down to the roots, and other suspect areas, where rampant, unpalatable grasses have taken over.

Before you do anything at all, get the soil tested to see whether it needs treating for imbalances or deficiencies. Samples should be taken from the good and poor areas of the field. Your local Animal Health Divisional Office (part of DEFRA in the UK) will be able to advise you on seed and fertilizer merchants who are qualified to carry out soil analysis. With a little effort, you can improve even the roughest pasture.

Harrowing and rolling

The regular use of a harrow can work wonders. Harrowing grassland in the spring – as soon as the land is dry enough – will have the same beneficial effect as raking a lawn: it will make room for new growth by removing dead matter, as well as aerating the soil. If there are badly poached (churned-up) places, these will need extra attention, especially if you want a level area on which to ride. The poached ground can be reclaimed by harrowing, re-seeding and rolling. Rolling the entire field in early spring (provided the ground is not heavy) can encourage early grass growth. If your soil test shows the ground needs fertilizing, harrow it before applying fertilizer.

Fertilizing

If your land has been well managed in the past, the soil may not require fertilizing. Applying too much fertilizer can be detrimental as it tends to produce over-lush grass which may lead to digestive-tract problems and even laminitis, a serious and painful inflammatory condition of the sensitive interior of the horse's hoof – ponies are especially susceptible.

If soil tests reveal a deficiency of any of the main elements required (nitrogen, phosphate, potash and lime), apply a suitable fertilizer in the spring, preferably while the field is being rested. The horses can go back on the land once the fertilizer has been washed into the soil or, if dry granules are used, when they are no longer visible. The grass will benefit from a further period of rest if this is possible.

Remedy acidic soil with a top dressing of lime. Have the land harrowed first and the lime applied on a still day to avoid wind-loss. Liming is best done in the spring or autumn. Keep your horses off the land until the lime has been washed in by rain.

If you prefer organic fertilizer, farmyard manure has the requisite nitrogen, phosphate and potash and is good for improving soil texture. To ensure it is free of infection, lay the manure aside for several weeks before spreading it and keep your horses off the treated field for several weeks afterwards.

Rotational grazing
The best way to prevent land from becoming over-grazed or 'horse-sick' is to divide it up so that some is resting while some is grazed. If you have two or more fields, you can graze and rest them alternately. If you have only one, use electric fencing to divide your land into grazing and resting sections on a rotational basis. If you have the space, divide it into three and put your horse in one section, leave another to rest, and put sheep or cattle in the other.

Grazing land for horses has to be kept in good condition. If you are unsure about which grass is best, check with your seed merchant.

Spraying

If some parts of your land have been entirely taken over by weeds, you may have to resort to spraying to kill them off. Take advice from a merchant and remember that there are specific laws which govern the use of weedkiller sprays. You can treat small areas yourself using a back-pack spray. For larger areas, you will need to bring in heavy machinery. You should apply the weedkiller in the late spring while the plants are growing strongly. If you are planning to use fertilizer, then it may be possible to combine the two applications. Always spray on a still day to minimize any drift.

If you do use a weedkiller, you must keep your horses and ponies off the land afterwards for the full amount of time recommended by the manufacturers. You should always bear in mind that horses are particularly sensitive to weedkillers, more so than farm animals, so always err on the side of caution.

Topping

Some fields need topping (mowing) during the summer to prevent the grass sward becoming leggy. Cutting helps prevent weeds and less palatable grasses from setting seed and spreading. It also encourages the more 'horse-friendly' grasses to grow. If it results in a lot of waste material, this should be raked up, removed and burnt, or it will inhibit the growth of the grass underneath.

Re-seeding

Where the grazing land has been neglected so badly that it is beyond repair, the only solution may be to have it ploughed and re-seeded. However, this option should not be considered lightly as your field may be out of action for at least a year. If possible, it is always better to improve what is already there.

Which grasses?

The beauty of re-seeding is that it enables you to start off with the best 'horse-friendly' grasses. Nowadays it is possible to buy some specialist equestrian seed mixes. A good basic horse mixture will include plenty of perennial rye grasses and fescues, plus other varieties, such as smooth-stalked meadow grass. If you have land from which you intend to cut hay, the mixture should also include Timothy. As with a garden lawn, the denser the grass sward to start with, the less chance there is of unwanted weeds getting in on the act.

Bear in mind that different types of soil will suit different grasses. For example, poor soil is no hindrance to crested dog's tail and common bent grass while dry, sandy conditions are tolerated by smooth-stalked meadow grass. Soil that is both rich and moist better suits the rough-stalked variety, which horses will find particularly palatable.

If the fertility of the soil needs improving, you can add a little wild white clover to the mixture. Its root nodules contain nitrogen-producing bacteria. However, never use the farm varieties of clover, as they will spread like wildfire and they can quickly overrun a whole field.

This all sounds complicated, but a good seed merchant will advise you. They will have knowledge of local conditions, such as altitude, rainfall and prevailing winds, all of which may determine which grasses will thrive in your particular area.

Drilling

Neglected fields can be reclaimed by direct drilling; you can hire a professional contractor to do this. If the soil is suitable, drilling can be a very effective way of improving bad pasture. It will create channels in the ground into which grass seed is sown together with fertilizer, as necessary. The land is then rolled. The seed will germinate most successfully when the soil is warm and moist, so spring or late summer is best for drilling.

Making your own hay

If you have a lot of land and the grass is suitable, consider using some of it for making your own hay. Bear in mind that you will not be able to use the land for grazing from around the middle of March until about six weeks after cutting. If the ground is wet, you may even need to rest it throughout the preceding winter.

Haymaking

The field should be harrowed and fertilized in the spring, and you will need to find either a local farmer or contractor to do the cutting and baling as it is not economical to buy special haymaking machinery for just a small acreage. There are two types of hay: meadow hay and seed hay.

• Meadow hay is always made from permanent grazing land which has had horses taken off it.

• Seed hay is made from fields which have been specially sown – the yield of hay will be heavier and of better quality than that from permanent pasture.

Horses and ponies will love the freedom of a large field or a paddock to exercise themselves. However, you must always check for poisonous plants.

Check for ragwort

It is essential when using land for haymaking and grazing to check that it is totally free of ragwort before cutting begins. Remember that this highly poisonous plant is far more palatable to horses when it is dry.

Check the drainage

If the field is drained by ditches, check them regularly to make sure they are working properly. If there are any obvious blockages, clear them out immediately. If the ditches are not blocked but the surface water is still not draining away, it could be they are blocked elsewhere – on the land of a neighbour, perhaps. If this is the case, you may have to do a little detective work in order to discover where the trouble lies.

Drainage problems can also be caused by damage to the structure of the soil, e.g., if heavy machinery is driven over the land while it is wet. If this is the case, get the soil professionally improved by breaking up the top layer. DEFRA can advise (see page 188).

Advantages

If you make your own hay, you will know it is good quality and will cost less than buying it. Your field will benefit, too, as good grass growth is encouraged and weeds are discouraged. Giving the field a rest from grazing will help reduce the worm burden.

Disadvantages

The downside of haymaking yourself is that finding a contractor can be difficult and they may not be able to do the haymaking when you want it done. Also, your horse may not like and eat hay that has been made from pastures grazed only by horses.

Worm protection

The best way to control worm infestations is to remove your horse's droppings every day with a wheelbarrow and 'poopascoop'. You can harrow the droppings on a regular basis if you can't pick them up but this is not so effective. Do not harrow in the wet: eggs and larvae thrive in wet conditions so harrowing will spread them over a wider area. Grazing cattle or sheep on horse pasture will help as their digestive system destroys the worm larvae.

Boundaries

Making sure that your horse is securely confined in a field or a paddock is very important. If he does get loose and causes some damage to property or injures someone, you will be liable. Always remember that a horse is, by nature, a nomad.

Stout three-bar fencing with the fence posts on the 'outside' of the field is expensive but ideal. You must regularly maintain the fence, repairing any broken sections quickly and weather-proofing the timber.

Fencing

Stout wooden post-and-rail fencing has traditionally been the material of choice for horse paddocks. Although the initial outlay may be high, when it is properly constructed and maintained, this type of fencing looks terrific and is long lasting, with a life expectancy of over 20 years.

However, it can be damaged by chewing, rubbing and leaning, and you should check it at regular intervals. Broken rails will need to be replaced promptly as the split timber and any exposed nails can be hazardous to horses. As always, some maintenance is required and the posts and rails will need regular creosoting to preserve them. Do make sure that the fence posts are sawn off at an angle, flush with the top rail, to avoid projecting posts that could cause damage if a horse tries to jump out.

Stud rails are an alternative and cheaper form of fencing. Made of plastic strips, they will withstand considerable impact, but they will stretch with time and require tightening.

Hedges

Hedges have one big advantage over fencing in that they provide shelter from the elements. However, they need to be really dense and strong (holly is particularly suitable) and, ideally, they should be free of any poisonous trees and shrubs. You must remove any poisonous growth by the roots if possible. Otherwise fence it off and keep it cut back so your horse cannot reach overhanging branches. Hedges will need regular trimming. Any gaps through which a horse could push his way must be blocked by strong fencing. Never be tempted to use a piece of flimsy wire which can cause severe injuries.

Wire

Wire in any form is not an ideal type of fencing for horses and should be avoided if at all possible. If it has to be used, then it needs to be kept taut and have a line of electric fence put in front of it. Wire mesh of any sort should not be used for horses.

Stone walls

Well-maintained stone walls make effective field boundaries for horses because they provide excellent shelter from bad weather and are stock-proof. They must, however, be kept in good repair and should be at least 1.2 m (4 ft) high – horses might try to jump out if they are any lower. If a wall is on the low side, you could consider fitting a rail above it or, in the case of cobs and ponies, one or two strands of well-tightened plain wire or an electric fence.

Electric fencing

This form of fencing is cheap and easy to erect. It can be used to keep horses away from a weakened fence or hedge; separate horses safely from others in adjoining fields; enable strip grazing of a field; or divide a field on a temporary basis in order to rest

Safety first
- Check any new fields for dangerous 'foreign bodies', e.g. lengths of wire, fragments of old farm implements, baler twine, etc.
- You should check on your horse regularly, preferably twice a day.
- Regularly inspect your field for rabbit holes, and fence off any areas that look unsafe.
- If your field adjoins roads or footpaths or has a path crossing it, check for litter. If it adjoins houses, check people are not dumping waste.

A metal sprung gate handle will require only one hand to open and close the gate.

Electric fencing can help prevent frisky horses jumping out of a field, although a few horses will not respect it and will still jump!

Padlock a remote or isolated field to prevent people accidentally leaving the gate open, and for your horse's security.

some areas. It should be positioned 1.5–1.8 m (5–6 ft) from the boundary fence, and it can be run off a portable battery-powered unit or wired up to the mains electricity supply with a transformer to reduce the voltage to approximately six volts.

Always avoid sharp corners and angles when you are erecting a fence, and never place it underneath or parallel to any overhead electric cables. The posts must be well heeled in, and any attachments to hedges and gate posts must have a sound insulator to break the current. The best electric fencing for horses is the thick white tape that is easy for them to see, cheap to purchase and simple to move.

Gates

Gateways need to be sited with care. In the interests of safety and security, avoid having a gate opening on to a busy road. However, bear in mind that you might occasionally need to turn large vehicles (such as a tractor with a harrow or roller attached or even, in an emergency, a horsebox or trailer) into your field. Make sure that the gateway is wide enough to take such machinery. Also avoid siting gates on any naturally wet ground – you should choose the driest spot possible.

Wooden or metal?

Both these materials are equally suitable for horse paddocks provided they are sturdily made, and both will need a certain amount of maintenance. Wooden ones should be treated with a non-toxic preservative, while galvanized metal ones need regular repainting. Rusty metal gates are dangerous for horses because they break easily and can cause serious injury. Never use narrow gates – with anything narrower than 1.8 m (6 ft) there is a danger of the horse bumping into the gateposts as it passes through. Horses' hips can easily be damaged in this way.

Installing gates

Always get the gateposts and the gates installed by a professional. A correctly hung gate will last for years and will be a pleasure to use. There is nothing more tiresome when you are leading a horse through a gateway than a gate that either flies open as soon as you unclip it, drags heavily on the ground and needs lifting, or swings shut of its own volition as you try to go through it.

Field gates are heavy and the posts that support them need to be sunk 90 cm (3 ft) into the ground. Really strong hinges must also be used, plus catches that cannot be opened by a horse with his teeth. Gates should be hung to open inwards, so when you go to feed or catch your horse he cannot barge through the instant you open the catch. Invest in strong metal chains and padlocks and affix one to the gate's opening side and another to the hinged side. You need to make things as difficult as possible for would-be thieves. If you must, in an emergency, climb over a gate, always using the hinge-end. Otherwise, avoid putting extra strain on your gates.

Feeding your horse

Always make sure you feed your horses well away from any gateways or the ground will soon become poached and getting in and out of the field in wet conditions will become really arduous. Having more than one gate will help.

A sturdy wooden gate, with strong hinges, which opens into a field is recommended. Note the white electric strip along the fence to protect the saplings.

Heavy-duty metal gates are suitable either with metal or with wooden posts. Treat them with a rust-resistant solution.

Water

A horse kept at grass needs constant access to clean water. His consumption may vary from as little as five litres (nine pints) a day to 45 litres (10 gallons) or more, depending on his size, the quality of the grass, weather conditions and time of year.

Buckets are easy to move about in a field, and this will prevent the ground getting poached.

Water containers

A galvanized metal or a concrete drinking trough, fed by piped mains water, is the most efficient method of providing water. Fit the trough with a ballcock to control the water level – enclosed to prevent horses from damaging it. Troughs should be set on a firm brick or concrete base and the area around may need firming by ramming hardcore into the ground.

However, if there is no piped water available, you can fill your container by hosepipe, assuming there is a conveniently located tap. If you only have to water one or two horses, you use buckets, old stone sinks

Siting water containers

- Site troughs lengthways along the line of a fence or at least 1 m (3 ft 4 in) away to prevent a horse becoming trapped between the trough and fence.
- Troughs recessed into the line of the fence can be used by horses in the adjacent field; a strong rail over the trough will stop them jumping over it.
- All water containers should be placed well away from any trees in order to prevent leaves and other debris falling into the water.
- Water containers should never be sited in the corners of fields because of the risk of a horse becoming trapped.

or plastic containers. These can be moved about the field to prevent the ground becoming poached but are knocked over easily and will need anchoring, e.g. by standing them in an old tyre. All containers that contain static water must be cleaned out regularly.

Keep any drinking troughs in your horse's field topped up regularly with clean, fresh water.

Natural water supplies

A stream or river in your field may seem like the perfect answer to your watering problems, but it is likely that the water, even if it looks clean, may be polluted. Unless you are absolutely sure that natural water really is pure, fence it off and provide your own supply. Fence off stagnant ponds and boggy areas, too. If a stream or river is clean, ensure the approach to the drinking area is safe. It needs to be fairly flat, as steep banks will eventually collapse. If your horse could wander along a watercourse on to someone else's land, erect a fence across it.

Shelter

In bad weather, horses like to take advantage of natural shelter, such as rocks or banks. In the heat of summer, they will take refuge under trees. Since many fields lack these facilities you may have to provide a wooden shelter, which affords the best means of escape from bothersome flies, or a windbreak screen.

Field shelters

Fields certainly provide a more natural environment, but the horses in them still need all-year-round shelter. Thick hedging can form a natural windbreak but, in many cases, the best option is a purpose-built field shelter. Again, you will usually find that you need planning permission for one that is sited permanently, although several companies now make 'portable' shelters that are said to be exempt.

If you have the option, site your shelter on the highest – and thus the driest – part of the field, so that the land surrounding it does not become waterlogged. The back should be facing towards the prevailing wind and there should be enough room between the shelter and the field fencing to prevent a horse being trapped by a more aggressive one.

Dimensions

These should always be a minimum of 5.5 x 3.65 m (18 x 12 ft) for two horses, and it is usually best to leave one side completely open so that both horses can come in and go out of the shelter without any problems: sometimes even good-natured horses will become bad tempered if they think that another horse is encroaching on their space.

Is your horse cold?
The best way to tell whether your horse is cold is to feel his ears. If they feel very cold, it may well be best to bring the horse into the stable and 'thatch' him. This involves placing a layer of straw along his back and putting a rug on top; this creates an insulation layer.

Structure and siting

If your horse or pony has one or more companions, then the field shelter must be large enough to accommodate them all without them squabbling. It should be open-fronted so that if a horse is picked on, he has a ready means of escape. To avoid the possibility of injury, there must always be plenty of head room, and, ideally, the roof should be sloped to the back to carry water away from the entrance.

Shelters should be strongly built and sited on well-drained ground to prevent the ground in and around them becoming poached. If this is not possible, you should provide a hard surface, such as concrete or hardcore, inside and in front of the shelter.

Position the field shelter with its back to the prevailing wind. However, remember to ask your local council first whether you need to get planning permission to erect a shelter.

Windbreak screens

Windbreak screens are much cheaper to build than field shelters and they can either be incorporated into the fencing or may be positioned in the open.

A field shelter should always be open-fronted to give the horse protection from rain and winds.

Know your poisons

Many trees, shrubs and plants are poisonous to horses. Learn to recognize them and check a new field before turning your horse out in it. If you find any poisonous plants, dig them up and burn them immediately. Trees and hedging material which are too big to be dug out must be cut well back and securely fenced off.

Beware!
There are many other poisonous plants that less frequently cause trouble for horses. If you are in doubt as to the identity and safety of any plant, you should take a specimen to your veterinary surgeon for identification.

Dead plants

Some poisonous plants, most notably ragwort and foxgloves, are more palatable to horses when they are dead, so never leave cuttings from any poisonous growth lying around. Inspect your land regularly; it may start off being poison-free, but toxic plants can spread all too easily from the adjacent fields.

Meadow plants

The most harmful meadow plants are ragwort, all the members of the nightshade family, meadow saffron, foxglove, hemlock, bracken, and monkshood. Aconite, bryony, flax, horseradish, hellebores, lupins, purple milk vetch, St John's wort, water dropwort and yellow star thistle are also dangerous.

Shrubs and trees

Poisonous shrubs include box, laurel, rhododendron and privet. Among trees, even a small amount of yew usually proves fatal. Keep horses away from laburnum, and take care with oak trees, whose leaves and acorns, if devoured in large quantities, are harmful. If there is a good crop of acorns, rake them up and remove from the field; alternatively, you could completely fence off the tree to prevent horses accessing them.

Poisonous vegetation

Acorns and crab apples Clear up and remove fallen crab apples from grazing pasture; they can cause severe colic. Acorns in large quantities are poisonous, but harmless in smaller amounts.

Bracken Horses eat this in late autumn or when other food is scarce. It has a chemical that destroys Vitamin B1. It usually has to be consumed over several months before producing any recognizable symptoms.

Deadly nightshade The brown or purple berries are poisonous. It grows in hedges on the edges of fields and should be pulled out and burned.

Horsetail The effects of this plant, which is also sometimes known as Mare's Tail, are similar to those of bracken. It is usually eaten in hay.

Milkweed, rhododendron and foxglove These contain chemicals that affect the heart and can cause sudden death in a horse. Dig them up and dispose of them.

Water hemlock and hemlock The symptoms of nervous system poisoning appear within two hours of being eaten by a horse.

Ragwort This will cause liver damage if consumed over weeks or months. It is usually found dried in hay, making it particularly dangerous. Its yellow flowers are in bloom between July and September, and mature plants can grow to a height of 120 cm (4 ft). You must pull up the plants and burn them.

Yew All parts of this tree are poisonous, even when it is dead. Just a handful of leaves, twigs or berries can lead to fatal effects for a horse within a matter of minutes. Always make sure that there are no yew trees bordering the areas where you turn out your horse to graze.

want to know more?
- For soil testing and analysis, contact your Local Animal Health Divisional Office (part of DEFRA) for advice
- Check with your local seed merchants about the best grass types
- For more information on ragwort, contact the BHS for their leaflet on the dangers of ragwort
- See the BHS leaflet on pasture management
- Ask your vet for advice on controlling equine worm infestations

weblinks
- Visit the BHS website at: www.bhs.org.uk
- Visit the DEFRA website at: www.defra.gov.uk

4 Safety and equipment

A basic knowledge of tack and equipment is essential, as the safety and comfort of you and your horse depend on it. Kitting out a new horse is a major expense, and you must work out what you need to get the best value for your money. Buying poor-quality equipment is dangerous as well as a false economy. It won't last and could literally put your life in danger. The fit is as important as function: a badly-fitting saddle may damage a horse's back, and a hat that is the wrong size will not give adequate protection.

Saddles

A saddle is the most expensive item of equipment that you will buy for your horse. There are three key points to consider: the saddle must be designed for the activity or activities you want to do; it must fit the horse; and it must fit the rider.

Synthetic saddles
Although these are much cheaper and usually lighter than leather saddles, it is just as vital that they are fitted and maintained by an expert, as even a lightweight saddle can cause muscle problems if it creates pressure points on the horse.

Saddle design

There are many saddle designs for the various disciplines, which range from dressage to racing. The basic differences between them lie in the cut of the flaps and the position of the stirrup bar. These factors will influence the stirrup length and also the riding position. For instance, a dressage saddle has a straighter flap than a jumping model and the stirrup bars will usually be set further back. This is because dressage, or schooling a horse on the flat, will involve a deeper seat and longer leg than other styles.

Usually the best choice is a general-purpose saddle, which gives support and allows you to school, hack out and jump to a reasonable standard in security. It has a forward enough cut to allow you to jump but is not so forward cut that you cannot sit in a more upright position on the flat.

Fit for the horse

It is crucial that a saddle fits well, or it will cause discomfort, pain or even permanent damage to the horse's back. Every horse should have its own saddle, with or without a tree – there are treeless saddles now – which is the correct width for the horse. It should always be fitted by a good professionally qualified saddler and should be checked and adjusted when necessary. Horses and ponies can change their shape as they gain or lose weight or as their muscles develop through work.

Every rider and horse owner needs to learn how to assess the basic fit of a saddle, and all this takes is some observation and attention to detail. It is essential that the saddle distributes your weight evenly and contours the back of the horse or pony so as not to inflict pain or discomfort.

If you start off with a well-fitting saddle which is the correct width for the horse and you check it thoroughly every month, you will know when there is a possible problem that will need professional attention from a saddler.

Parts of the saddle

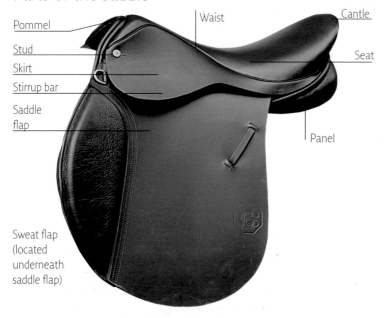

Pommel

Stud

Skirt

Stirrup bar

Saddle flap

Sweat flap (located underneath saddle flap)

Waist

Cantle

Seat

Panel

Basic points to look for

If you are considering buying a saddle, whether new or second-hand, you should consider the following:

- The saddle should always be level from the front to the back and the rider should be balanced – neither tipped forwards nor backwards.
- It should sit evenly on the horse, not to one side.
- The gullet should clear the horse's back all the way along, especially when the rider is mounted.
- The panel should always be in contact with the horse, without pinching it anywhere.
- The pommel should clear the withers; the cantle should clear the back. The clearance needed depends on the work you are doing. Stand in the stirrups and ask a helper to put two fingers between the pommel and the horse's withers. If their fingers get pinched, then the saddle will come down too low as you ride.
- When you ride, your saddle will move slightly with the horse, but there should not be any rocking, either from side to side or backwards and forwards, and the back of the saddle should not bounce up and down.

Mounting

Using a mounting block rather than mounting from the ground will help prevent the saddle from being pulled over to one side, which is uncomfortable for the horse and may lead to the tree of the saddle becoming twisted over a period of time. Saddles are very expensive items and it thus is well worth looking after them.

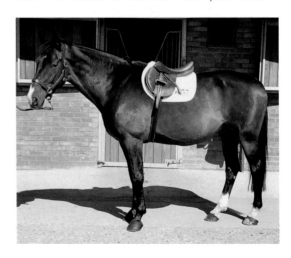

When you are choosing a numnah or saddle pad, it is wise to get expert advice before you buy one.

Fitting a saddle

A correctly fitted saddle will spread the rider's weight properly over the horse's body. This is essential both for your horse's health and your own safety. You should always ask a member of the Master Saddlers Association to fit your saddle for you. A comfortable saddle that fits properly and conforms to the horse's shape is a must if you want your horse to perform well and also to avoid some of the most common fitting problems.

The tree of the saddle (with the front arch) must conform exactly to the horse's shape, as shown here, so as not to inflict pain or discomfort and to avoid pressure.

Fit for the rider

Although priority will be given to fitting the saddle to the horse, it is important that it also fits the rider and encourages a correct, balanced position. A rider who is off-balance will be an uncomfortable burden on the horse. Therefore you must also check out the following points carefully before you make your final decision on which saddle to buy.

This saddle is too wide. If your weight is over the front arch, the saddle drops to the wider part of the horse and the frame lifts off at the back, transferring your weight to the front.

• The saddle seat will need to be large enough to accommodate the rider comfortably without putting pressure too far back on the horse, as can happen in the case of a large rider who tries to ride a horse or a pony that is too small for them.

• The saddle flaps should be the right length for you: if they are too short, they will catch on your boot tops. However, if your thighs hang over them at the back, then your security and comfort will be affected when you are riding.

• The knee rolls should be sited so that when your stirrups are adjusted correctly, your knee sits just behind them. Some saddles have movable knee rolls, which are fastened on with a special sort of Velcro to allow you to customize the fit.

After riding and removing the saddle, if it is fitted correctly, the hairs of the horse's coat along its back should lie in a natural line. This can be checked easily.

Saddle fittings

In addition to a good well-fitted saddle, you will need some fixtures and fittings, such as stirrup leathers and irons and also a girth. Again, these should be the best quality that you can possibly afford and they should always fit correctly.

It is important to saddle up your horse correctly and check that the girth is tight enough to keep the saddle in place when riding.

Stirrups

These should be made from stainless steel for strength and must be the right size for the rider. When the widest part of your foot rests on the tread, there should be 1.25 cm ($^1/_2$ in) clearance either side – no more, or your foot could slide too far in to the stirrup, and no less, or your foot could become trapped. Most riders use rubber treads for extra comfort and security.

Safety first

Many saddles still have stirrup bars (metal fixings that hold the stirrup leathers in place) with traditional hinged ends. These must always be pushed down and must allow the leathers to slide off when they are pulled hard. In the event of your foot becoming trapped in a fall, the leathers will be released.

Safety stirrups

Those with rubber rings on the side are fine for lightweight small children, but older youngsters and adults tend to use the 'bent leg' designs where the metal takes the stress of heavier weights.

Always run the stirrups up the leathers when you are leading or holding a tacked-up horse; this will prevent them flapping about or getting caught up. Never lead a horse out of the stable with the stirrups down, or they could catch or bang on the door. If you lunge a horse with the saddle on, secure the run-up stirrups with the leathers turned up. Pass the end of the leather through the loop before slotting it through and securing the loop on the flap. Use an overgirth or elastic surcingle to prevent the flaps flying up and down.

Stirrup leathers

These are made from leather or synthetic materials. Most riders put more weight in one stirrup than the other, so if the leathers have the capacity to stretch it is a good idea to swap them round each time you ride to try and keep them even. Regular riding lessons will help you to keep your position and weight level.

Girths

Girths can be made from synthetic materials or leather. Those that 'give' a little as the horse breathes out are presumably more comfortable for the horse. Leather girths, in particular, are often shaped behind the elbow, where the skin is thinner than in many other areas and therefore more prone to rubbing. Girths must be kept clean to ensure that they do not rub and chafe your horse, causing 'girth galls'.

Numnahs and pads

Numnahs and pads come in many designs and materials, including sheepskin, cotton and even models incorporating airbags. Some are said to relieve pressure or help prevent the saddle slipping. Ask your saddle fitter's advice if necessary and make sure that whatever you use stays up in the saddle gullet and does not pull down on the withers, leading to rubs or pressure points.

Stirrups

Irons

Peacock irons

Rubber quick release

Rubber treads

Numnah

Putting on a saddle

Before you saddle up your horse, collect everything that you will need and have it to hand. Tie up the horse securely (the rope should not be too tight nor too loose) and talk to him soothingly.

Saddling up your horse

Start by checking that the stirrup irons are run up, the numnah or pad is pulled up into the gullet, and the girth is folded over the saddle seat.

Lower the saddle gently well forward of the horse's withers, and slide it back into the correct position so that the coat hairs on the back of the horse lie flat.

Go to the other side of the horse to release the girth so that it rests down the horse's side. Check that all is safe under the saddle flap. Go back to the near (left) side, reach under the belly and fasten the girth, loosely at first. Tighten, a hole at a time, until it's tight enough to keep the saddle in place but does not cut into the horse. Check it again before moving off and after riding for a few minutes. Now gently pull each foreleg forward in turn to release any wrinkled skin.

Before mounting

Before you mount, always double check that the bridle, bit, saddle and numnah are all adjusted correctly. It is better to be safe than sorry.

1 Approach the horse's nearside, talking gently all the time. Make sure he is tied up securely. Place the numnah or saddle cloth well forward over the horse's back and smooth it out.

2 With the saddle in your right hand, place it on top of the numnah, pulling the numnah up into the gullet. Slide the numnah and saddle back together into the correct position.

3 Check again that the numnah is positioned well up into the gullet of the saddle. Go to the horse's offside to check the girth.

4 Reach down and do up the girth on the nearside. Fasten the back girth to the third girth strap and then adjust the buckle guard.

5 Next pull the buckle guard down over the buckles to prevent them moving and rubbing, damaging the saddle or rubbing against your legs when you are riding.

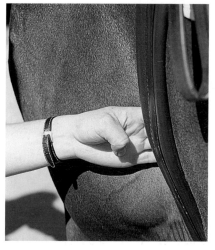

6 Give the girth a final check to ensure that it is tightened correctly and that no skin is wrinkled below. You don't want the saddle to slip round when you are mounting.

Putting on a saddle | 79

Removing a saddle

If the saddle is dirty and is spattered with mud after riding, it is always the best policy to clean it immediately as any mud will come off more easily if it is sponged while it is still wet.

Putting the horse away

If the horse is wet, after removing the saddle put on a sweat rug or place some straw underneath the rugs and walk him dry. Pick out his feet; wash them if they are muddy. Check his legs and sponge or brush off any sweat marks. Groom him, checking for telltale signs of rubbing in the saddle, girth and mouth areas. Put him back in his box, tie up the haynet and refill the water bucket or trough. Replace all his rugs before bolting the door.

1 As soon as you dismount, tie up the horse securely and run up the irons on the leathers.

2 Your next task, while you are still standing on the horse's nearside (his left side), is to unfasten the girth.

3 If the girth is wet or muddy, leave it down; otherwise, you can put it over the top of the saddle by going round to the offside.

4 Lift the saddle and numnah, sliding slightly backwards, then drawing them gently off and placing them on your right arm.

Bits and bridles

The right choice of bit and bridle is vital for a horse's comfort, to enable him to work correctly and for the rider to control him. As with saddles, bridles must always fit correctly.

Bits

There are literally hundreds of types, but they can be divided into groups. For most riders, the important ones to know about are: snaffles, with a single rein; double bridles, which have two bits and two reins; and pelhams, with bits that can be used with a single or double rein and are more severe than a snaffle. All bits rest on the bars of the mouth and, depending on their design, act on some combination of the bars, tongue, corners of the lips, curb groove and poll. Their purpose is to help you control your horse.

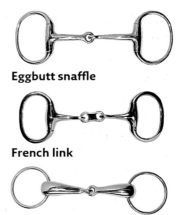

Eggbutt snaffle

French link

Loose-ring hollow mouth snaffle

Snaffles

These are simple to use and fit, and most horses that have been correctly trained go well in them.

• The eggbutt snaffle will stay still in the horse's mouth and the smooth sides will minimize the risk of pinching. It's a good bit to discourage horses that are 'mouthy' and tend to play with the bit.

• The loose-ring snaffle will make constant tiny movements in the mouth and encourages a horse who is 'set' in his mouth to relax his jaw.

• The French link snaffle has a less direct action and many horses like it.

• The three-ring snaffle is potentially a powerful bit; the rein can be fixed to any of the rings and the lower it is, the greater the possible leverage and control.

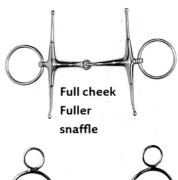

Full cheek Fuller snaffle

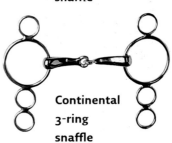

Continental 3-ring snaffle

Mullen-mouth pelham

Pelham roundings

Double bridles

This comprises two bits: a thin snaffle with small rings called a bridoon and a curb bit with cheekpieces of varying lengths called a Weymouth. The Weymouth is fitted with a curb chain, which rests in the horse's curb groove and applies pressure when the curb rein is used. With a double bridle, an experienced rider can establish good communication with a well-schooled horse. However, it should not be used by inexperienced riders or on horses that are not well established in their basic education.

Pelhams

Pelhams try to combine the action of a double bridle in one mouthpiece and are used with a curb chain. They act on the poll and curb groove as well as on the mouth. There is a wide range of mouthpiece designs and materials, and many horses go well in them.

Ideally, a pelham should be used with two reins; the one on the top, or 'snaffle' ring, gives less leverage than the one on the bottom, or 'curb' ring. At first, holding two sets of reins and using them independently of each other may seem confusing for the rider, but the skill will come with plenty of practice and the help of a good instructor.

Some riders will prefer to use a single rein and couplings, which are called pelham roundings and are attached to the top and bottom rings. This is quite a popular option for jumping.

The Kimblewick also has a curb chain and is less subtle in its action than a pelham. It has a single rein and is another bit that acts on the curb groove and poll. Nowadays, it is not seen as often as it used to be, as a horse tends to set its jaw against the action.

Fitting a bridle

In order for a bridle to fit correctly, the different components must be the correct proportions for the horse's head and they should be adjusted so as not to pinch or rub anywhere.

Guidelines

The main things to remember when ever you are fitting a bridle are as follows:

- The headpiece and browband must not pinch the horse's ears.
- The throatlatch (pronounced 'throatlash') must not be too tight.
- The noseband must not rub the facial bones and, if it fastens below the bit, it must not interfere with the breathing or be so tight that it prevents the horse mouthing on the bit and flexing his jaw.
- The reins must be long enough to allow the rider to lengthen and shorten them, but not so long that there is a danger of the rider's foot catching in the loop. This can happen if children on smaller ponies ride with reins designed for horses.

Types of bridle

A snaffle bridle is used with one pair of reins. Many riders like to use different designs of reins to give a better grip, such as ones made from laced or plaited leather or those that incorporate rubber or other synthetic handgrips. Double and pelham bridles are used with two pairs of reins, usually plain leather with the top rein wider than the bottom one. Some riders like top reins made from laced or plaited leather or with rubber grips inside.

Neckstrap
If your horse does not wear a martingale (see page 84), it can be a good idea to use a neckstrap, especially if he is young and/or lively. This gives you something to hold on to if he misbehaves. A simple method of making a neckstrap is to buckle a spare stirrup leather round his neck.

Martingales

These give you extra control. In common use are running, standing and bib martingales. They should be fitted in such a way that they are just tight enough to prevent a horse raising his head above the point of control but not so tight as to hold the head down. Running and bib martingales attach to reins; standing ones to a cavesson noseband or the cavesson part of a flash. Never use it with a drop noseband, or it will affect the horse's breathing.

Bridles and headcollars can be leather or synthetic. Leather looks best for bridles, but washable synthetic designs can be useful for muddy conditions. Leather headcollars are better than nylon ones, which can be used in situations where a horse is under supervision.

Safety

For safety, use a leather headcollar when travelling, and a leather or 'safety' design with a breakaway section to prevent the horse getting caught up out in a field. However, it is better to turn out a horse without a headcollar on. Designs marketed as 'pressure' or 'controller' headcollars should only be used by experienced riders and never for tying up a horse.

On the nose

The simplest type of noseband is a cavesson, which fits under the bridle's cheekpieces giving a 'finished' look to the horse's head. Many horses will perform well in a plain cavesson noseband and a snaffle bit.

Different types of noseband are used to give more control, usually by preventing the horse from opening its mouth too wide and/or crossing its jaw, and by applying pressure to the nose. Flash nosebands are most commonly used but drop and Grakle (crossed) nosebands are suitable in some cases. However, the cavesson is the only noseband that should be used with a double bridle or pelham.

Breastplates

Breastplates and breastgirths are used to prevent a saddle slipping back, especially in cross-country competition. However, they are not an adequate substitute for a correctly fitting saddle.

Checking the fit

It is important for the comfort of the horse and your safety that the bridle fits correctly – neither too big nor too small, too loose or too tight. It is easy to check whether a bridle is fitted correctly as is shown below. The best bit is the one that is kindest in allowing the horse to go forward under your control; the type used will depend on the horse's schooling and temperament.

Above: If you cannot put a finger or two into the noseband, it is too tight.

Left: There should be 5 mm (¹/₄ in) between the side of the mouth and the bit.

You should be able to fit two fingers between the browband and horse's head.

Your hand should always be able to fit sideways under the throatlatch.

Insert your hand under the headpiece to check that the horse's mane is flat.

Putting on a bridle

A bridle must always fit properly and effectively. It should be kept in good condition not only for the horse's comfort and wellbeing but also for your safety as a rider.

Checking the fit

- The browband must not be too tight or it will pinch the ears; too loose, the headpiece may slip back.
- The cheekpieces should be an even height on both sides, with the buckles just above eye level.
- The snaffle bit should slightly wrinkle the corners of the mouth and not protrude more than 5 mm (¼ in) each side.
- Buckle the throatlatch so you can insert four fingers between the leather and the horse's jaw.
- The noseband should be two finger widths or 2.5 cm (1 in) below the cheekbone. Allow at least one finger's width between the leather and the horse's jaw when it is fastened at the back.
- The reins should have 43–51 cm (15–20 in) spare when held.

Guidelines

Check the noseband and throatlatch are undone. Put the reins over the horse's head and, if tied up, loosen the quick-release knot and remove the headcollar. Fasten the headcollar round his neck. Hold the bridle in one hand and support the bit with the other. Present the bit to the horse's mouth gently; many will take it of their own accord. If not, press lightly on the bars with your thumb.

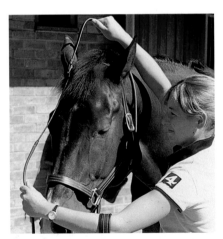

1 Approach your horse, talking to him gently, and then slip the reins over his head. Undo the headcollar and put it round the horse's neck.

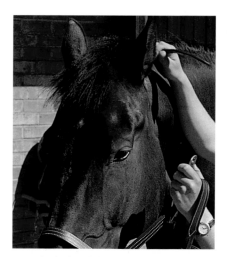

2 Undo the headcollar and then put it round the horse's neck. Fasten it to ensure that you have control of the horse.

3 Hold the bridle in one hand in front of the horse and, with the other hand, guide the bit into his mouth without banging his teeth.

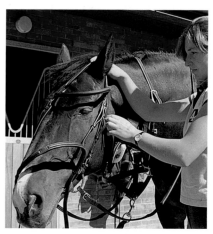

4 Bring the headpiece up over one ear and then over the other ear. Make sure that you tidy the mane under the headpiece and pull out the forelock from the browband.

5 Do up the throatlatch, leaving space for four fingers to fit between the cheek and strap. The noseband should be taut – to put at least one finger between the nose and the leather.

Rugs

Rugs have many uses: providing protection from the weather, when travelling, drying off a wet or sweating horse, and keeping the back muscles warm and dry when exercising in bad weather.

Which size rug?

To find out which size, measure from the centre of the horse's chest along his body to an imaginary perpendicular line dropped from the top of his tail. Most rugs fasten at the chest with cross surcingles under the belly; there should be one hand's width between the surcingles and the horse. A well-fitting rug will come just in front of the withers, will fit at the neck and chest without gaping or pulling tight and will not restrict the movement of the horse's shoulders.

Types of rug

• Turn-out (or New Zealand) rugs are waterproof, breathable and lightweight. They are worn by horses living out in winter, and by stabled horses that are turned out during the day.

• Stable rugs keep a stabled horse warm at night. They can be hemp, canvas, jute or synthetic.

• Summer sheets are lightweight, usually cotton. They keep a horse's coat clean, protect against flies, and are used for horses travelling to competitions.

• Outdoor fly rugs protect against flies and insects.

• Thermal rugs and coolers will help dry off a wet or sweating horse.

• Exercise rugs keep a horse's back warm and dry.

Comfort and safety

A rug should be deep enough to cover the belly, elbows and stifles, and sufficiently long to cover the dock and buttocks. It should fit over the shoulders, withers, ribs and croup. It should fit snugly around the neck. If too loose, it may slip back over the withers and cause a sore. Also, the horse might get a foot caught in the neck when he is getting up and tear the rug or injure himself. If the rug is too tight in the neck, it may put pressure on the windpipe. Horses with high withers may benefit from rugs fitted with comfortable sheepskin pads inside part of the neck.

Putting on a rug

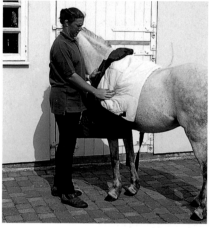

1 Fold the back of the rug in half (with the lining facing outwards) and approach the horse or pony at the shoulder.

2 Gently put the folded rug on the pony, talking reassuringly to him, with its forward edge well in front of the withers.

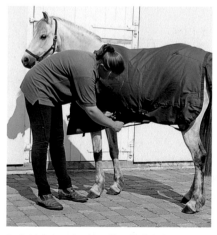

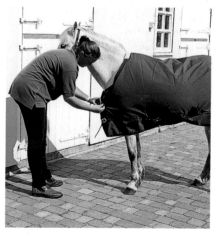

3 Fold the rug back, pulling it slightly towards the rear, and then fasten the belly straps without pulling forwards.

4 Fasten the front straps without pulling the rug forwards, then go behind the pony and fasten the hind leg straps by linking them.

Booting up

Boots are worn to protect horses' legs, especially when they are jumping or travelling. You should use them when working young or unbalanced horses or ones that tend to brush or overreach.

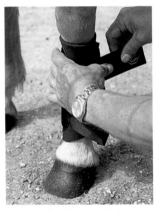

Fasten the straps of the boot on the outside of the leg, taking them from front to back.

Boots should not be too tight. You should be able to slip a finger down inside them. These are a bit too long, as shown.

Types of boot

Most boots are designed so that each fits snugly on a particular leg, though some of the latest brushing boots can be used on any leg. They must be the right size and adjusted so that they stay in place without putting any pressure on bones or tendons. The most commonly used boots are the following:

• Brushing boots protect the inside of the cannon bone and fetlock if the horse brushes (hits one leg with its partner on the other side).

• Overreach boots protect the front heels from being struck or trodden on by a hind hoof.

• Tendon boots protect the tendons down the back of the front leg from being struck by a hind hoof.

• Travelling boots prevent the horse from knocking his limbs when he is travelling. Some are designed to protect the limbs from the knees and hocks down to the coronary bands. Bandages can be used instead but boots will save you time and labour.

General handling

When you examine your horse stand close to him. The closer you are to the hind leg, pressing on it, the less risk of being on the receiving end of a kick. Get your horse accustomed to being touched: regularly run your hands over his head, neck, body and legs. This helps detect any abnormal lumps and bumps.

Bandages

Bandages are used to protect a horse's legs from injuries and to keep the tail tidy and protected when travelling. There are several types but it is important to apply them correctly. Badly applied leg bandages can do more harm than good to a horse's legs and may actually damage them.

Leg bandages

These can be used to protect your horse's legs, either when he is working or travelling, to keep an injury clean, or to give warmth and support. Before using them, it is very important that you learn the correct techniques for bandaging.

Stable bandages

These protect the horse's legs, provide warmth, keep the circulation active and help to dry off wet legs. They are useful to support the opposite leg of a horse that injures a leg and consequently puts more weight on the sound one. Travelling bandages are similar to stable bandages but tend to come lower down the leg to ensure protection for the coronary band. Exercise bandages for working horses should only be applied by experienced owners who have expertise in bandaging techniques.

A tail bandage should be firm but not pulled too tight. The tapes should not be tied tighter than the bandage itself. Make sure that you only leave it on for a few hours as it can cause discomfort.

Surgical bandages

These bandages cover and protect wounds and they are usually made of a synthetic stretch material. Special cohesive bandages, where each wrap sticks to the one underneath, are often used over dressings or poultices.

Always put a layer of padding under a bandage. Check that it fits well and that it lies smoothly before covering it.

Make sure that you have the bandage ready and firmly rolled before you begin to bandage your horse's legs.

Tail bandages

These are used in the stable to keep the tail tidy and to prevent the tail hair being rubbed when travelling, perhaps with a tailguard on top for extra protection. They encourage the hairs in a pulled tail to lie flat.

Putting on bandages

Bandaging is a skill that will take practice and the best way to learn is to get someone experienced to show you how to do it. The vital points to remember when bandaging are as follows:

• Leg bandages should always be used over padding.
• Do not wet bandages, or they will tighten on the limb or tail as they dry.
• The tension should be even and the bandage should not be too tight – as firm as necessary to keep it in place and prevent it from slipping.
• Fastenings should be secured on the outside of the leg so they do not put pressure on bone or tendon.
• Bandages should be rolled firmly and applied without any wrinkles.

Bandaging

Applying a stable bandage must be done properly so as not to damage the horse's legs. Start with the bandage rolled with the tapes or fastening inside the roll. Put the padding round the leg. Holding the end of the bandage against the leg with one hand, go round and round with the other hand, overlapping each turn by at least half to two-thirds of the breadth of the bandage. Always bandage from the front to the back of the leg. Finally, tie the bandage around the leg with a neat, tight bow on the outside and tuck away the loose ends.

Putting on a bandage

1 Hold the end of the bandage with one hand and then slowly begin to unroll it around the horse's leg, pressing firmly.

2 Start at the top of the padding and then work downwards. When you reach the bottom of it, you should go back up again.

3 Each turn should overlap the previous one by two-thirds of the breadth. The lining should show at least 1 cm ($^1/_2$ in) above and below the finished bandage.

4 Fasten the bandage with the same tension, either with tapes or some Velcro. You should be able to slip a finger down inside the bandage. Fold in the tapes.

Looking after tack

It is very important that you look after your tack and equipment and check it regularly for any signs of wear and tear. Get into the habit of running a quick visual check over it before you get on a horse, whether it is your own or someone else's.

Looking after and cleaning your horse's saddle is a really important task not only for its appearance and durability but also for safety reasons.

Tack

Check stitching regularly, especially on reins, girths, girth straps and stirrup leathers, for signs of wear and get any repairs made immediately. Keep a close eye, too, on areas where the metal rests on leather.

In an ideal world, where our time is limitless, tack is taken apart and cleaned thoroughly after every use. However, as long as mud and sweat are wiped off after riding and the tack wiped over with a cloth that has saddle soap on it, a thorough clean once a week and an occasional 'feeding' with a good leather dressing will be sufficient to keep leather items supple. Only if the leather is encrusted with heavy mud should you use a wet cloth and water – too much water will cause leather to become hard and brittle. Use a dry cloth or chamois leather to dry it off.

Cleaning a saddle

Put it on a saddle horse, with the girth, leathers and stirrup irons on hooks. Next wash the leathers, girth, stirrup irons and treads. With the saddle up-ended, rub the underneath clean with a damp cloth. Rinse the cloth and clean the rest of the leatherwork. Do not over-wash any clean leather, such as the seat of the saddle. Rub the saddle soap with brisk circular movements into the flaps, girth and leathers. Do not put too much saddle soap on the seat and flaps. You must also clean the irons regularly. Use a dry cloth to buff stainless steel irons and clean with metal polish. Nickel stirrup irons should not be used. If a saddle has been used only on a clean horse with a numnah, it will not need frequent cleaning, but the girth and leathers should always be cleaned carefully after use.

Leather girths should be soaped or oiled after cleaning; nylon, string, webbing or lampwick girths may be brushed clean if dry, or soaked in warm detergent and then scrubbed if muddy or stained. Hang them up to dry by the buckle ends.

Synthetic tack should be cleaned according to the manufacturer's instructions. Some is designed to be wiped clean whilst other products can be washed in a domestic washing machine.

You should always use a sponge or cloth when transferring saddle soap to the tack.

Rub in the saddle soap with brisk, circular movements. Be sparing and don't use too much.

Rugs

Clean according to the manufacturer's instructions. Using a thin, easily-washed cotton or thermal rug under a bulkier one will help to keep the lining of the thicker rug clean to prevent frequent washing.

Before rugs are put away in store, they must be washed or cleaned or the ingrained manure will rot the material. Before washing, oil all the leatherwork or remove the fittings and sew them back on later. Put more oil on the leatherwork and buckles after washing. Hang rugs up to dry thoroughly before putting them away. Webbing rollers and surcingles should also be washed at home. Do not soak leather fittings in hot water or they will become brittle and break; they should be oiled regularly. Leather rollers should be washed clean and then treated with neatsfoot oil or leather dressing.

Riding clothes

You, like your horse, need to be equipped for comfort and safety, whether you are schooling at home, hacking out or competing. Every rider can find something suitable, regardless of age, size and personal taste, but the golden rule is that you must wear proper headgear every time you get on a horse.

Hard hats and helmets

No matter how well you know the horse, how quiet it seems and how short a time you will be out riding, it is essential that you wear a hard hat or helmet that meets the most up-to-date safety standards, fits properly, is adjusted correctly and has not suffered an impact. If your headgear receives a blow, which

Even when you are riding at home or hacking out, you should be suitably dressed and always wear a hard hat or safety helmet, proper riding boots and gloves.

usually happens if you have a fall or are kicked, throw it away and buy a new one. You must never buy a second-hand hat; the protection it offers may have been compromised by a previous wearer's fall even if there is no outward damage.

For most people, the best way to buy a hard hat or helmet is from a retailer who is a British Equestrian Trade Association member and who has attended its course on fitting hats and body protectors. Someone with this experience will also be up to date on the latest safety standards.

For everyday use, you can choose between a velvet-covered hat or a safety helmet. Helmets are available with a wide choice of features, including really bright colours, ventilation slots and washable linings. It is also sensible to wear protective headgear whenever you are lungeing or clipping a horse, as well as when you are riding. In some cases, such as when you are handling a young horse, it is safer to wear a hard hat or helmet at all times.

Footwear

Proper footwear keeps you safe and comfortable not only when you are riding but also on the ground in the yard, field or stable. The one time that you decide to take a chance and lead your horse to the field wearing a pair of soft shoes is the time that he will stand on your foot!

Leather boots will give you more protection than rubber riding boots but, if you are on a tight budget, rubber ones are absolutely fine. However, they must be made specifically for riding; it is not safe to ride in Wellington boots, as the heavily-ridged soles may lodge in the stirrups.

The comfort zone
You cannot ride well if you are uncomfortable, so stretch jodhpurs or breeches are better than trousers. Don't wear jeans; the inner seams will rub your legs. Wet-weather gear is a great investment, and many riding jackets are machine washable and smart enough to wear when not riding. Follow the manufacturer's care instructions for washing and cleaning high-tech fabrics. Waterproof chaps or overtrousers make riding in the rain much more bearable.

Body protectors
Wear these when you
are jumping or riding
cross-country. They
must be fitted and
adjusted correctly. It is
sensible to wear one
whenever you are riding
a young or excitable
horse, even if you are
schooling or hacking.
If a horse is nervous of
being clipped, a body
protector offers some
protection from kicks.
Even an experienced
handler can be caught
unawares by a quick
'cow kick,' when the
horse kicks forward.

Long leather boots look good but are expensive
and they are often kept for competition use. For
everyday use and also for young riders who are still
growing, short boots, either the traditional jodhpur
boots or ones that zip up, are often a much better
option. They can be teamed up with half-chaps or
gaiters which are designed to give the appearance
of long boots and which can give you extra support
and protection.

Boots that are designed specially for use on the
yard may not be suitable for riding, again because
of the construction of their soles. In both cases,
it is possible now to buy designs with safety toecaps
which will minimize the risk of injury if a horse steps
on your toes; again, a good specialist retailer will be
able to help you to choose some boots that meet the
latest and most appropriate safety standards.

Gloves

These are another simple safety precaution. They
should always be worn for riding, lungeing and when
leading a horse. Modern designs mean that there are
gloves for all weathers and jobs: stretch cotton with
grip palms are comfortable in warm weather and
lined leather or synthetic materials are suitable in
less pleasant conditions.

Be seen, be safe

Riders need to be seen to be safe, all year round.
In the UK, BHS statistics show that there are at least,
on average, eight horse-related accidents a day, with
no difference between summer and winter accident
rates. Research shows that motorists spot riders and
horses that are equipped with reflective fluorescent

You and your horse must be
easily visible to motorists and
other road-users when you are
out riding on the road.

Note the difference between the rider on the left wearing high-visibility clothing and the rider on the right who is merging into the dusk and is hardly visible.

equipment three seconds earlier than those in 'plain clothes'. As braking distance at 60 mph (40 km/h) on a dry road is 74 m (240 ft), wearing high-visibility gear can help to save lives.

There are many products now available, including rugs, boots and rider clothing. Research for the BHS has shown that the combination of a fluorescent, reflective hatband for the rider and boots all round on the horse make a very effective combination. The rider's head can be seen at high level and the horse's movement is immediately eye-catching.

Riding in rain and poor light is inevitable for most of us. This is when materials that are reflective and fluorescent are best, as they show up in headlights. They should also be used when you are leading a horse on the road – for example, when you are taking him to or from the field.

want to know more?
• Contact the Society of Master Saddlers to get a saddle fitted correctly
• Ask your vet or an experienced person to show you how to bandage legs correctly
• Check whether the local saddlers offer rug washing services
• For hard hats and helmets, check that the retailer is a British Equestrian Trade Association member on: www.beta-uk.org

weblinks
• Visit the BHS website at: www.bhs.org.uk
• Visit the Society of Master Saddlers website at:www.mastersaddlers. co.uk

5 Handling your horse

Building a good partnership with your horse means paying as much attention to the way in which you handle him as you do to your riding skills. The keys to success in communicating effectively with him are being consistent and kind, coupled with firmness, patience and establishing mutual respect. These ground rules will always apply, whether you are dealing with an experienced horse with a quiet temperament or one that is more sensitive and quick to react.

Think like a horse

The biggest compliment you can pay a rider is to say they are a true horseman or horsewoman. Some people have more of a natural affinity than others, but handling skills can be learned and they will grow with practice and confidence.

The horse's eyes are widely set and positioned on either side of the head, giving him a wider field of vision than humans. A horse's expression is the key to its temperament and it should be bold and generous.

A horse's senses

These are honed towards survival. Horses can hear things from much further away than we can and can also hear sounds in lower and higher registers. As a prey animal, a horse has eyes that are set at the side of his head (as opposed to us, who, as hunters, have them set in the front). This gives the horse a much wider field of vision than us, but it has to alter its head position to see things that are near or far away.

The power of the voice

Horses are very responsive to the voice, when it is used correctly. If you babble away, a horse will often switch off, but a soothing word will help calm an excitable or worried animal, and also keep you calm.

Any horse can learn simple verbal commands, but your tone is vital: a drawn-out word ending on a descending note will have a slowing down or soothing effect whilst a quicker command ending on an upward note will encourage him to go forward.

Whenever you are going to approach or touch your horse, speak quietly to him first so he knows you are there. If his attention is elsewhere, touching him without warning may startle him. Be polite in the same way you expect someone to be polite to you. A quiet 'Good boy' is the equivalent to someone saying

'Excuse me' before approaching you, rather than marching up and prodding you in the back.

It is said that horses can smell fear. This may be true to the extent that fear stimulates the production of adrenaline and alters your body chemistry and smell, but it also means that if you use techniques, such as deep breathing, and keep your muscles relaxed rather than tense, your horse will pick up on your state of calmness and be reassured by it.

The learning process

Horses learn through positive reinforcement and repetition, whether they are being handled or ridden. You must set the ground rules and see that you both stick to them. No matter how stressed or fed up you may be, you need to switch on your calmness and concentration before you go near your horse.

Positive reinforcement

Reinforcement must be positive, not negative. If you punish your horse for shying when you are leading him, you are carrying out negative reinforcement by confirming there is something to be frightened of. Similarly, a quiet word of praise and a scratch on the neck will confirm that he has done what you asked.

Correcting your horse

There will be times when you need to correct your horse, but this must be done immediately, so that he associates the correction with what he has just done – never in temper – or the horse will not be able to associate it with the behaviour it relates to. At the subtlest level you can correct a horse by repeating an instruction that he has ignored or misunderstood.

Body language
Horses are responsive to body language, which means we have to be, too. Used in the right way, body language can help you to handle a horse more easily, but if you inadvertently take the wrong stance, you may have problems. Squaring your shoulders, making yourself look as big as possible and looking a horse directly in the eye makes it move away from you; lowering your gaze and turning away encourages it to come to you, because it will not feel threatened.

Putting on a headcollar

As long as you do it the right way, most horses are reasonably easy to catch (see opposite). Unless there are any special circumstances, they will usually not be wearing a headcollar.

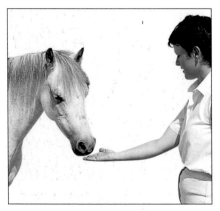

1 Approach from an angle, calmly and quietly, and talking gently to the horse, with the headcollar hidden behind your back.

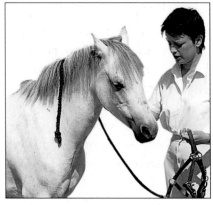

2 Pass the lead rope round the neck to keep control if necessary. Bring the headcollar slowly up to the face – not in a rush or jerkily.

3 Gently slide the noseband up over the muzzle. Keep talking to him quietly while you do this to put him at his ease.

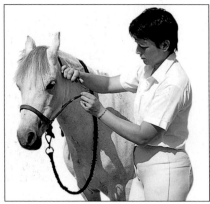

4 Do up the head strap and check all the parts of the headcollar are properly seated and not too tight nor too loose. Tidy the mane.

Catching a horse

Like children who enjoy playing outdoors, there are some horses and ponies who would sometimes prefer not to be caught, and it may take you some time and effort to do so.

Guidelines

If you get your horse used to coming to you to be fed or talked to and patted, catching him will not be a problem as he will learn that being caught leads to a treat. Never chase or corner your horse. He will enjoy the game and will be much quicker and more nimble than you. Instead, be patient and offer him rewards in the form of carrots or mints. Always praise him and fuss over him when you succeed in catching him.

1 Enter the field and approach the horse at an angle to his shoulder, holding the headcollar behind you so he cannot see it.

2 Talking gently to him all the time, approach the horse steadily and run your hand down his side.

3 Put the lead rope around his neck and raise the noseband over his muzzle. Slide on the headcollar.

4 Adjust the head straps so that the headcollar fits properly, and then pat and reward the horse.

Leading a horse

It is very important that horses are handled equally from both sides, not only from the traditional near (left) side. Not only is this safer and more convenient for you as the handler, but it also helps to ensure that the horse is always comfortable and controllable wherever the handler is positioned.

Turning a horse
You will often have to turn a horse in one direction or the other, especially if you are checking it over for soundness. As with everything to do with horses, there is a way to make this as safe as possible. Look carefully at the photographs opposite to see the correct way to turn your horse or pony.

Basic guidelines

To lead a horse in a headcollar in the accepted way, you should stand at his shoulder. If leading from the near side, your right hand will hold the lead rope near his head, close enough to the clip to give control but not so close that his natural head movement is restricted, whilst the free end rests in the other hand. Do not ever put your fingers through the headcollar rings or wrap the rope round your hand; if the horse spooks or takes off, you could be injured.

Look ahead and then take a step forward, if necessary giving a short verbal command to your horse such as 'Walk on'. An educated horse will keep pace without pulling. To turn him, move the hand nearest his head slightly away from you so that the horse also turns away. Turning him away from, rather than towards, you will lessen the risk that he will tread on you.

Sometimes, you will need to lead a horse in a bridle. If this is the case, always pass the reins over his head and position your hands in a similar way to when you are leading him on a headcollar rope. However, you should separate the reins with your index finger to give you more directional control.

Leading a horse through a gate

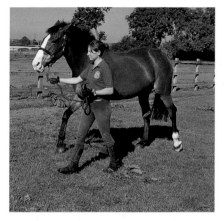

1 Encourage your horse to walk forward towards the gate out of the field – talk gently and reassuringly to him. When turning your horse, you should always hold the headcollar or bridle quite close to the mouth.

2 Turn the horse away from you. You may get trodden on if you try turning him towards you. He will have to bend his neck as you turn his head away from you. He will then walk beside you through the open gate out of the field.

Turning out a horse

1 To bring your horse back into the field and let him loose, you must lead him in hand through the open gateway to the field. Talk to him reassuringly.

2 Make sure you close the gate behind you. Turn the horse so his head is at the gate with his body straight behind. Quietly undo and take off the headcollar.

3 Pat the horse, but do not turn your back on him. You need to keep a careful eye on him to ensure that he does not turn quickly and kick up his heels.

Tying up

Whenever your horse is taken out of his stable to be groomed, shoed or clipped, or for it to be mucked out, he needs to be tied up securely. Always use a quick-release safety knot.

Safety guidelines

Tie the lead rope to a loop of strong string or sisal baler twine, rather than directly to a tying-up ring or rail where the string could break and he could end up trailing a piece of broken wood at the end of a flapping lead rope with the obvious potential for injury.

1 Start off by putting the loose end of the rope through the string.

2 Make a loop with this piece of rope close to the string.

3 Put this loop across and on top of the other part of the rope.

4 Hold the loose end near the loop; pull it through the loop to make a 'U' shape.

5 Now you should pull the rope really taut.

6 Put the loose end through the loop to complete the quick-release knot.

Picking up feet

Before you ask a horse to pick up a foot, check he is standing with his weight evenly distributed so he can adjust it easily as he needs to. Use a simple verbal command such as 'Up'.

Picking up the front feet

Remember when approaching your horse to speak gently and reassuringly to him in the usual way to put him at his ease. Start at the shoulder and then run your hand down his body to his foot.

1 Speak to your horse, then touch or pat him on the shoulder so that he tunes in to your presence and stays relaxed; if you simply take hold of his leg, he may not be properly prepared. Run your hand down his foreleg.

2 Keeping in contact with him, run your hand down the back of his leg, towards the outside rather than the inside, until you reach the fetlock. Meanwhile, talk reassuringly and quietly to him all the time.

3 A gentle squeeze will encourage the horse to lift his leg for you and you can then either hold the fetlock or grasp the foot a little lower down. Make sure that the horse is tied up or held by someone while you do this.

Picking up a hind foot

1 Approaching from the horse's head, run the hand nearest to him along his back and then down his hindquarters and outside of the leg to the hock.

2 Keep your hand on the outside; when you reach the hock or halfway down the cannon bone, run it down the front of the hind leg to the fetlock.

Establishing a routine

If you always move round the horse and pick up the feet in the same order, he will soon become accustomed to the routine and will often do it for you without you having to do any more than support the toe as he lifts a foot off the ground.

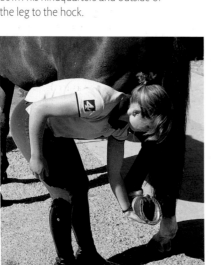

3 Now squeeze the fetlock, lifting it forwards and upwards so that the leg joints bend, and then catch hold of and support the hoof rim.

Safety measures

Whatever you do with your horse, whether you are leading him or riding on the roads, safety must always be a high priority, for your sake and that of other people around you as well as for your horse. Just a few seconds spent putting on a pair of gloves, for instance, could stop you from getting rope burns later on.

Safety on the ground

More horse-related accidents happen on the ground rather than in the saddle, and many of these mishaps can be easily avoided just through taking some common-sense safety measures, such as those that are outlined below.

• Never take a horse for granted, no matter how well you know him. For instance, the quietest pony may spook if a bird flies out of a hedge when you are leading him, so always be aware of your surroundings.

• Don't get sloppy because you are short of time. The day on which you take your horse down to the field in soft shoes rather than boots offering greater protection is the day that he will tread on your foot and leave you with broken toes.

• Always wear gloves and a hard hat when leading, long reining, lungeing or loading a horse. Never wrap ropes or reins round your hand or you run the risk of being injured or dragged.

• If you are clipping a horse that might be ticklish, wear a hard hat, especially when you are bending over to deal with the belly and legs.

• Never kneel down at the side of a horse; always crouch down, so that you can jump out of the way if it is necessary to do so.

Be courteous
It is vital that you show courtesy to other road users whether you are riding or leading a horse on the road. If drivers slow down or give you priority, always thank them. It is not always safe to take a hand off the reins to signal your thanks, but it should always be possible to smile and to nod to indicate your gratitude.

Road safety test
The BHS riding and road safety test will reinforce the need for observation and show you how to make motorists aware of your intentions. Your local BHS Riding and Road Safety officers will help you prepare and take the test. All the issues relate to the Highway Code, such as observation, signalling, your positioning at road junctions, roundabouts, passing stationary vehicles and coping with hazards.

Testing times

Most riders will have to ride on roads much of the time but there are still many motorists about who do not understand the nature of horses and the fact that even the quietest ones can occasionally behave unpredictably and out of character. Riders would also do well to remember this and not fall into the trap of ignoring what is going on around them. One of the best ways of appreciating the skills and techniques of riding on the road is to take the BHS riding and road safety test (see box left).

Passing stationary cars

1 As you approach a car that is parked on the side of the road, always look behind you to check whether any other road users are approaching. Both you and your horse should be wearing high-visibility equipment – this is an essential all year round, not just in rain and gloomy conditions.

2 Signal your intention to move out around the stationary vehicle only when it is safe to do so, and then take back the reins. Do not attempt any manoeuvre with only one hand on the reins as you will not have sufficient control of your horse.

3 After checking the road is clear ahead and behind you, move the horse out to go round the car. Allow enough space between the horse and car to ensure that a driver who starts approaching from behind will not try to overtake when there is not enough room.

4 As soon as you can do so safely, move back to your correct position on the road. If you are leading, in order to put yourself between the horse and the traffic, you will have to lead from the off (right-hand) side. The horse will see you more and the traffic less.

Grooming basics

The amount of grooming that an individual horse needs will depend on his regime and how much work he is doing. A horse kept at grass and not working will need minimal grooming.

When to groom

The accumulation of grease and dirt in a horse's coat is nature's way of helping him to stay warm and dry. However, if you ride your horse off grass, you will need to tidy him up before putting his tack on. Removing the worst of the mud and cleaning and checking his feet will probably be sufficient. After exercise, make sure that he is quite cool and dry before turning him out again into his paddock.

A stabled horse should be groomed before and after exercise. Beforehand he needs a quick brush over or 'quartering'. Immediately after exercise, when he is still warm and the pores of his skin are open, he should be groomed thoroughly.

Tying up your horse

Before grooming, always tie the horse up, using a headcollar and rope. Use a stable ring fixed to the wall but never tie the rope directly to the ring; attach a loop of string to the ring and attach the rope to that (see page 108). If you tie the horse directly to the ring and he takes fright and runs back, he may break his headcollar or slip and injure himself. Always tie the rope with a quick-release knot (see page 108). Put the end of the rope through the loop to deter the horse from undoing it with his teeth. Never use a frayed rope because it may not come undone easily.

Safety first
- **When brushing legs, crouch down so you can get out of the way quickly if the horse moves suddenly.**
- **When brushing his hindlegs, stand close to your horse's body and use one hand to hold his tail while you brush with the other. This helps to steady a restive horse and you can also feel if he shows any signs of flexing his hock with the intention of kicking.**
- **Never stand directly behind a horse; you might get kicked.**

Equipment

Dandy brush

The long, stiff bristles will remove dried mud and sweat. The dandy brush may be used on the horse's body if he has not been clipped, but it is too harsh for a thin-coated horse, one that has sensitive skin, or for use on the horse's head. It is not suitable for the mane and tail as it will break the hairs.

Water brush

The bristles of the water brush, which are shorter and softer than those of a dandy brush, are used for dampening the mane and tail. It can also be used to remove stable stains (where a horse has lain in its droppings). You can use a dry water brush to remove any mud and sweat from a sensitive-skinned horse.

Metal curry comb

The teeth of the metal curry comb are used for cleaning the body brush. You simply draw the brush over the teeth after every few strokes and tap the dirt out of the curry comb at regular intervals well away from the horse. The metal curry comb should never be used on the horse.

Sweat scraper

The scraper's rubber blade, which is attached to a metal frame fitted with a handle, is used to remove excess water from the horse's coat after he has been washed down. Be very careful when working round the horse's bony areas.

Mane/tail combs

These metal or plastic combs are not required for grooming but they are essential items when you want to pull (thin and trim) or plait your horse's mane or tail.

Body brush

The short, fine bristles of the body brush can be used all over the horse, including his legs, head, mane and tail. It is fitted with a loop through which you can slip your hand.

Plastic curry comb
The teeth are suitable for removing dried mud from the coat of an unclipped horse.

Rubber curry comb
Use for removing mud, sweat and any loose hairs and for massaging the horse.

Cactus cloth
The coarse-weave cactus cloth, which originates from Mexico, can be used instead of a plastic curry comb for removing mud and sweat.

Hoof pick with brush

Hoof pick

Bucket
A bucket is useful for washing your horse's feet, and wetting sponges and water brushes. Never use his drinking water for such purposes.

Hoof pick
The hoof pick, which must have a blunt end to avoid causing injury, is used to clean soil, droppings, stones, etc. from the horse's feet.

Sponges
These are used for cleaning the horse's eyes, nostrils and dock (area under his tail). Always keep separate sponges for the head and dock.

Stable rubber
A cloth stable rubber is used slightly damp to remove the last vestiges of dust from the horse's coat and give it a final gloss at the end of grooming.

Other equipment
There are also some other items of equipment that might prove useful when grooming your horse, and these include the following

Pulling comb
This is used both to tidy and shorten manes and strip out long hairs.

Hoof brush
A small brush to get into the grooves of the hoof.

Hoof oil brush
This is good for painting on hoof oil.

Quartering stabled horses

This is done in the morning and takes about 15 minutes, depending on the size of the horse and how dirty he is. Some horses lie down at night more than others; some have the unhelpful habit of always choosing the dirtiest part of their bedding.

How to groom
You will soon develop a routine to suit you and your horse. Grooming is a good opportunity to check for warning signs of health problems and build a good relationship with your horse.

Basic guidelines

A rugged-up horse is groomed a quarter at a time. Do this before exercising him; it only involves picking out his feet, brushing off any stable stains with either a sponge or water brush, sponging the eyes, nose and dock, and brushing the mane and tail. If the horse is dirty, you may also need to wash clean any specific areas and then towel them dry. When you are doing this, you should pay special attention to the hocks, knees, flanks and under the belly.

1 Start by picking out the horse's feet into a bucket (not into his bedding). Use a hoof pick from the heel towards the toe, taking care not to damage the sensitive frog.

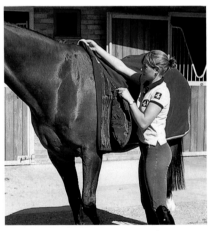

2 Next unfasten the rug and turn it back carefully over the horse's loins so that you are in a position to give each side of his front half a quick brush over.

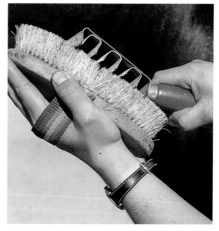

3 Brush the horse's coat lightly with a body brush. Use a brush or a damp sponge to remove any stable stains and then dry off with a cloth or towel.

4 Afterwards you must remove any stray hairs from the body brush to keep it clean by regularly drawing it over the teeth of a metal curry comb.

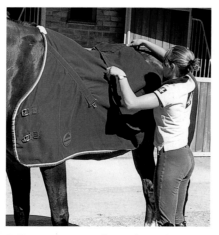

5 Now you can turn the rug forwards over the horse's withers and start brushing his hindquarters with the body brush.

6 Always make sure that you brush in the direction of the lie of the horse's coat. Lastly, brush out the mane and tail.

Grooming stabled horses

A stabled horse will usually also need a full grooming session as well as quartering. This will remove any dirt, sweat and waste products from his coat and help to massage his muscles as well as his skin.

Safety guidelines

When grooming a horse, always face his quarters, never away from them. Do not stand directly behind him or you may receive a shove or kick! Groom your horse outside the stable where it is less dusty.

Before you start grooming, always put on a headcollar with a rope and tie up the horse, using a quick-release safety knot. Never tie him directly to the stable ring.

Pre-grooming clean

1 Start by removing any mud from the horse's coat with a rubber or plastic curry comb. Brush in firm strokes with the dandy brush.

2 Beginning at the horse's neck and working downwards, rub in circular motions with the curry comb.

Checking the hooves

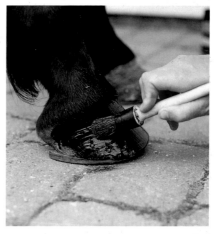

1 Pick out the sole of each of the horse's hooves. Remove any foreign bodies and check the frog. Look for any smelly areas of rot.

2 For special occasions, you can paint on some hoof oil in order to keep the wall of the hoof strong and in good condition.

Grooming the mane

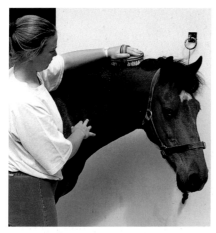

1 With the body brush, brush the mane over to the other side so that the brush goes right through the hair down to the roots where grease can accumulate.

2 Brush the mane back over again to the original side, a little at a time. Next, brush the horse's tail, standing to the side of the horse. Brush gently, a section at a time.

Using a body brush

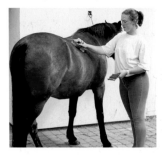

1 Start at the top of the neck and work down in the direction of the hair with straight movements.

2 After two or three strokes, scrape the brush on a metal curry comb to clean out the bristles.

3 Tap the curry comb on the floor to loosen any hairs frequently during grooming.

Useful tips

• Never try to groom a sweaty horse. If the weather is suitable, walk him about after exercise until he has dried off.

• Speed up drying-off a wet horse inside his stable by covering him with a sheet that is made of breathable material. A traditional method is to place a layer of straw along his back and hindquarters with an inside-out rug over the top (thatching). The rug keeps him warm; the straw absorbs moisture and allows air to circulate.

• In cold weather, keep a thin-coated or clipped horse warm while grooming by turning his rugs back and then forward, as in quartering (see page 116), rather than removing them totally.

• Wash grooming tools in detergent regularly. To prevent the bristles becoming loose, avoid over-wetting the backs of brushes and lie them on their sides to dry, away from direct heat.

• Get your horse accustomed to being hosed by trickling water gently around and over his front feet. Gradually work up his legs and on to his body. Only increase the water pressure when you are sure that he is not frightened. Most horses will accept being hosed and even seem to enjoy it in warm weather.

Sponging the head

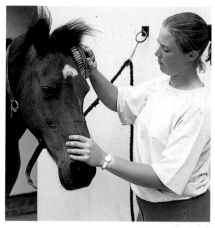

1 Put the headcollar round the horse's neck before brushing the head. Note that the lead rope should be through the string but not in a quick-release knot.

2 With the body brush, gently brush the face, steadying the head with one hand. Do not forget to brush under the jaw and gullet and around the ears. Do not be rough.

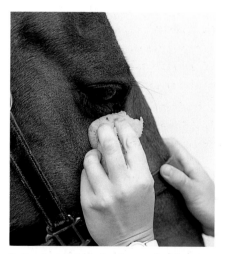

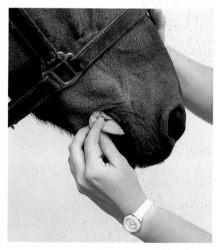

3 Put the headcollar back on and, with a damp sponge, which is kept specifically for this purpose, sponge the eye area with some clean, preferably warm, water. It should not be so wet that it gets water into the horse's eyes.

4 Rinse out the sponge in some clean water and then gently but firmly sponge around the horse's muzzle, mouth and nostrils, rinsing the sponge as required. Remove any discharge from around the nostrils.

Washing the dock

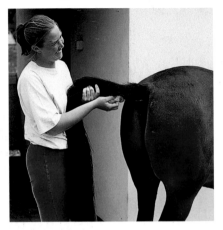 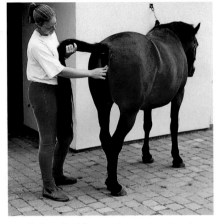

1 With another damp sponge kept for this purpose, gently sponge the dock (the skin at the top of the tail and above the anus). Stand to one side of the horse while you do this.

2 Lift the tail while you clean around and sponge the area underneath. It is best to keep a second sponge specially for this task. Take care not to muddle up your sponges.

Laying the mane

Polishing

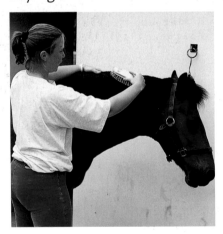 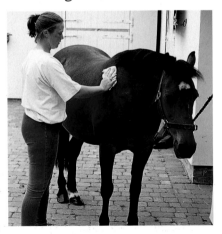

Using a damp water brush, brush the mane downwards from the roots to the ends of the hairs, stroking the hair into place. This makes the mane look neat and tidy.

Finally, use the stable rubber all over the body to 'polish' the coat and give it a healthy, glossy finish. Always wipe the horse's body in the direction in which the coat lies.

Sponging and washing

A very sweaty horse, after hard exercise, may be sponged over once his breathing has returned to normal (he will need to be walked about until he has recovered from his exertions).

Weather conditions

If the weather is hot, use cold water or a hose pipe to clean and cool the horse off. In cold weather, use tepid water. Never use hot water: the horse may get a chill. A sweat scraper will remove surplus water. If it is warm, walk him about uncovered until he is dry. In colder conditions, cover him with a cooler rug, kept in place by a roller and breastplate, or use thatching (see page 120).

Washing manes

Wet the mane well (including the forelock) with a sponge and warm water, and then work in the shampoo before rinsing well, especially the roots. Remove excess water from the neck with a sweat scraper and dry his ears with a towel. Finish by brushing the mane out gently, a section at a time, with a clean body brush.

Washing tails

Use a wet sponge to clean the dock (the top, bony section) and then immerse the long hair in a bucket of warm water. You may need an assistant to stand at the horse's head and to steady him for you. Rub shampoo into the tail hairs and dock area.

Rinse the whole tail thoroughly in several buckets of clean water. The best way to remove the excess water from the long hair and to dry the tail is to stand beside the horse, with your back towards his head, then grasp the long hair just below the end of the dock and swish it swiftly round and round. Finally, brush the tail hair out carefully with a clean body brush or, if the tail is quite thin, with your fingers.

Gently wash off any dirt, mud and stains on the horse's legs with a water brush. Only give your horse an all-over wash on a warm day.

Neat and tidy

In addition to grooming and washing your horse, you may need to trim and pull his tail and mane occasionally, especially if you are planning on showing him or competing.

Pulling the tail will neaten the top and will also help to keep it looking tidy.

Pulling manes

A horse's mane can be kept neat and manageable by means of 'pulling', which involves plucking out a few strands of hair at a time until the mane is the desired length and thickness. Like humans, some horses are more sensitive than others, so you should be prepared to work on only a small section of mane at a time, taking several days to complete the job. It will be easier and more comfortable for the horse if you pull his mane when he is warm – after exercise while the pores are open. However, if he will not tolerate having his mane pulled, you can tidy it up with a thinning comb, not scissors.

Hogging manes

You can improve the appearance of a really thick, unmanageable mane by removing it altogether. This is called hogging and is done by running the clippers up either side of the neck, starting from the withers. It looks best on a heavily built horse such as a cob. To stay neat, it will need hogging every few weeks.

Pulling tails

Pulling is also used to neaten the top of the horse's tail (the dock) if it is bushy and untidy. As with the mane, pulling the tail should always take place when the horse is warm and should never be rushed, otherwise the dock may become very sore. Only small amounts of hair are removed, mainly from the sides. After pulling, you should apply a tail bandage for a few hours to encourage the hair to lie flat.

To avoid being kicked if the horse objects to having his tail pulled, hold the tail over the stable door (with an assistant holding the horse's head). With a very sensitive-skinned horse, it is kinder and safer to leave the tail as nature intended and for smart occasions simply to plait it.

If your horse lives at grass it is best to leave his tail unpulled, since the hair helps protect the dock. It is customary with finely bred horses, like Thoroughbreds, and some breeds such as Arabs, to leave the top of the tail in its natural state. Damping down the hair will be sufficient to keep it looking neat and tidy.

Shortening tails

To shorten the length of a horse's tail, raise his dock to the position where he normally carries the tail when he is on the move. Hold the hair at the end of the tail with your other hand and then cut to the required length. The end of the tail should be parallel to the ground when the horse is moving. For safety reasons, always use blunt-ended scissors for this.

Ears and legs

To keep a stabled horse looking smart, the long hair that grows round the front edge of the ears and around the heels and the fetlocks may be trimmed off. To trim an ear, hold it closed with one hand and use the scissors from the base of the ear to the tip. The internal hairs provide protection from dirt and insects and thus they should never be removed.

Heels and fetlocks can be trimmed with blunt-ended scissors. It takes practice not to leave unsightly 'steps', so take your time. If your horse has large quantities of feather (leg hair) you may need to use the clipping machine fitted with a special leg blade, which is designed not to crop the hair too short. Remember that with some breeds (e.g. native ponies) it is traditional not to remove feather. If your horse lives out, he should always be left untrimmed in winter as the hair gives protection from the weather.

Clipping

The thick coat a horse grows in winter can cause problems if he does anything other than light work. He will sweat excessively, lose condition and could even end up with a chill if he is not dried off thoroughly after exercise. Clipping solves this problem.

Take care
Be careful when clipping delicate places, such as round a gelding's sheath or between the forelegs and round the stifle. Straighten out the folds of skin in these areas with your spare hand. To clip behind the elbow and between the front legs, get your assistant to pull each front leg as far forward as it will go and keep it stretched out by clasping their hands round the fetlock. A haynet will help to distract the horse while you clip.

Care of clipped horses

If you clip off some or all of a horse's coat, make up for the loss of his natural protection by covering him with rugs to keep him warm when he is not working. A horse that is clipped, or partly clipped, and spends some of his time out at grass will need a waterproof and windproof rug which is specially designed for outdoor use. A New Zealand turn-out rug is ideal.

Types of clip

The amount of hair you remove will depend on the type of coat your horse grows and the work he is doing. A full clip involves removing the coat from his whole body and legs. It is often a good idea to give a thick-coated horse a full clip the first time and then leave the hair on his legs at subsequent clippings to afford him some protection against any knocks.

The frequency of clipping depends on how quickly his coat grows. Some horses will need clipping every two to three weeks; other more finely coated ones might go for four weeks. The first clip is usually done in October when the horse's winter coat is through.

The usual type of clip used for horses in hard work is known as a hunter clip. It involves removing all the coat except for the legs and saddle patch (the latter helps prevent sore backs).

For horses doing medium to hard work, a blanket clip may be suitable. This leaves an area of the back, loins and quarters unclipped, plus the legs. Horses that are stabled but not in hard work, or are living outside, can be trace clipped, i.e.removing the hair from the underside of the neck, between the forelegs, the belly and upper part of the hindlegs.

How to clip

1 Mark out the lines, e.g. the saddle patch and tops of the horse's legs, with chalk or damp saddle soap.
2 If you are using a mains hand clipper, assemble the machine, and check the cable and plug. Plug it in to check that it is working properly. Switch it off and then put it in a safe place out of the horse's reach.
3 Start clipping on the horse's neck or shoulder, then work your way back over his body and hindquarters.
4 Always use the clippers against the lie of the coat and keep each stroke parallel to the one that is above or below it and slightly overlapping the previous one.
5 Take great care when you are clipping the top line of the neck as you do not want to clip into the mane.
6 Finish the top of the tail with an inverted 'V'.

Clipping the head

A horse that is disturbed by the noise or vibration of the clippers should have his head left unclipped. Remove untidy long hairs around the jaw with scissors and a comb and leave the edge of the ears. When clipping the head, use the clippers lightly to reduce vibration. Be especially careful when working round the eyes and never clip the eyelashes. Many people just clip half the head as far forward as the protruding cheek bone.

Nervous horses
If your horse is nervous, he may be less worried if you use a battery-operated clipper, which is quieter and vibrates less than an electric clipping machine. However, clipping an entire horse in this way is very time-consuming as the clipper will over-heat more quickly and you will have to keep stopping. If a horse is dangerous to clip, you may have to resort to sedation (your vet will be able to advise you).

Plaiting

A mane and tail may be plaited to make the horse look smart for showing, competing and special occasions. An untidy mane on a stabled horse can be tamed by putting it into long plaits.

Plaiting tip
To make an unruly mane lie flat, divide it up, then make loose plaits and secure the ends with rubber bands. There is no need to roll them up. Re-plait the mane on a daily basis. The plaits need to be fairly tight if they are to stay in place, but beware of making them so tight that they cause the horse discomfort; he has to stretch his neck when he is working.

How to plait a mane

To plait your horse's mane for, say, going to a show, you will need a comb and a water brush, a small bucket of water, some rubber bands or a needle and thread (choose a colour that tones in with the mane) and a pair of scissors. If necessary, you should find something solid on which you can stand, such as an upended box, so that you can reach the horse's mane comfortably.

Number of plaits

It is customary to have an uneven number of plaits along the horse's neck but the total number can be varied. Note that a short neck will look longer if you use lots of small plaits, whereas a long neck will look shorter if you use fewer plaits. You can help to disguise a ewe-neck on a horse by making the plaits in the dip of the neck a little larger than the rest.

Sewn plaits or rubber bands?

Sewn plaits are the most secure and should be used for lengthy periods of work, such as hunting. They will look better if the thread does not show. If the mane does not have to stay plaited for long – for example if you are going show jumping – rubber bands will suffice. Again, use a colour that matches the horse's mane.

Plaiting a mane

1 Start off by very gently brushing or combing the horse's mane to tease out and get rid of any tangles without hurting him.

2 Divide the mane into as many bunches as are required, and then you can separate each bunch into three equal strands.

3 Next, taking the three strands in one bunch securely in your fingers, you can plait down as far as possible.

4 Use a rubber band in a matching colour to secure the end of each plait, or take a needle and thread and sew it firmly.

5 Turn the plait under and secure with a rubber band, or, alternatively, stitch each turn so that it is firm without any loose ends.

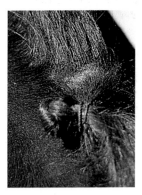

6 The rubber band or thread should be neatly visible only at the top end of the plait. Proceed in the same way down the horse's neck.

How to plait a tail

If you plan to plait your horse's tail for a show, you will need to have some long hair at the top of the dock, so always make sure that you leave it unpulled. It is much easier to plait a tail that has first been washed and then well brushed through.

There are two methods of plaiting a tail: you can either use a simple flat plait, as is shown here, or a more complicated ridge plait which will require more skill, patience and plenty of practice.

1 Start the plait by taking a few hairs from either side of the top of the dock and some from the centre.

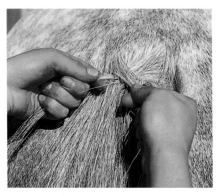

2 These are the three locks of hair that make the plait. Now plait them together and work down the tail.

3 As you work your way downwards, each time take a few more hairs from the sides.

4 Continue plaiting, gradually taking a few more hairs from each side as you go down.

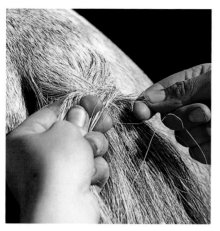

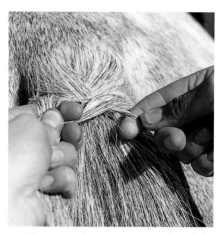

5 As you can see here, no more hair is taken from the centre of the tail, just a few hairs at a time from the sides.

6 This process may seem fussy and will take a little time but the plait will soon become evident and will look tidy.

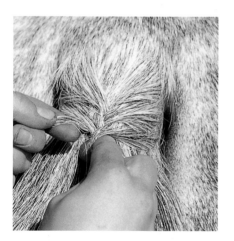

7 When you are two-thirds of the way down the dock, you should continue without taking any more hair from the sides.

8 Keep plaiting until the end of the plait is reached, then stitch the end, double it underneath and stitch again.

Shoeing

The outer horn of a horse's foot is constantly growing, and the hooves need protection if the horse is not to become lame which is why man has been shoeing horses with metal shoes for more than 2,000 years.

The modern farrier is a highly skilled craftsman and you should make regular appointments with him to check your horse's feet.

Regular attention

Whether your horse is exercised regularly or is unshod and turned out to grass, its hooves need regular attention and trimming to prevent them growing too long and becoming misshapen. Most horses need their feet trimmed once every four to six weeks. The farrier removes the shoes, trims off excess horn and, if the shoes are worn, puts on new ones. If the old ones are not very worn, they may be refitted.

Fitting the shoes

Shoes can be fitted hot or cold. The benefit of hot shoeing is that the shoe (which is bendable when hot) can be finely adjusted to the shape of the horse's foot for a better fit. The shoe is heated and placed in contact with the insensitive underside of the hoof for a short time. The imprint it leaves shows the farrier whether further adjustments are needed and if the sole is flat. Once the farrier is happy with the fit, he plunges the shoe into cold water before nailing it into place. The nails are driven up into the insensitive wall of the hoof, the points protruding through the wall. These are twisted off to form clenches, which prevent the nails from being pulled back through the hoof.

The role of the farrier is a crucial one, as there is little room for error when shoeing horses since the inner structures of the foot are highly sensitive.

Checking the feet

Check your horse's feet every day and, if shod, ensure his shoes are not loose or the clenches raised above the level of the hoof, which can cause injury to one of his other legs if he strikes himself. If in doubt, call the farrier.

Diet is important

A stabled horse on a balanced diet or a horse turned out on good pasture should be getting all the essential vitamins and minerals required for the production of strong horn growth without any help from you. However, some horses on a good diet will still have weak and brittle hooves. Your farrier or veterinary surgeon will be able to advise you on a suitable additive or ointment, if it is required.

Oiling the feet

Special hoof oil can prevent the feet from becoming too dry. Oiling of the wall helps prevent undue evaporation, but don't overdo it, particularly around the coronary band and on the sole. Too much oiling can be counterproductive and can cause brittle feet as it prevents the natural absorption of moisture.

Inspecting the feet

Whether your horse is shod or unshod, you need to inspect his feet on a regular basis. The hooves of unshod horses need to be checked carefully, and any small flints or debris that could cause lameness must be removed. They should be looked at by your local farrier and trimmed as necessary to prevent the hoof wall cracking.

want to know more?
- Contact the local BHS Riding and Road Safety Officer for information on the BHS riding and road safety test
- Find out about farriers in your area from the National Association of Farriers and Blacksmiths at: www.nafbae.org.uk
- Ask your vet for advice on food supplements to combat hoof problems
- To learn how to clip, enrol on an equine short course for novices. See the website at: www.hartpury.ac.uk

weblinks
- Visit the BHS website at: www.bhs.org.uk
- Visit the Driving Standards Agency website at: www.dsa.gov.uk

6 Feeding and diet

Horses are continuous 'trickle' feeders and have a comparatively small stomach capacity. Over the years, they have adapted to compound feeds, but with so many feeds on the market and so much controversial information, feeding horses can become a headache for many owners and carers. This chapter gives you an insight into the digestive system of the horse, the various feed types available, and the role they can play in his diet. Even experienced owners may struggle to devise feeding regimes that are suitable for each individual horse on their yard. If you are in doubt, seek advice from a qualified nutritionist or vet.

The rules of feeding

All owners should adhere to the following rules when feeding a horse. They should be used not only as guidelines when you are devising regimes but also as daily good hygiene practice. The rules are in no order of priority, but are equally important.

If your horse is living out, he may only need extra food when the quality of the grass is poor. Be sure to keep an eye on him and check the grazing.

Feed good-quality feeds

Feeding inferior quality feedstuffs, such as dusty hay, could result in health problems, including COPD and colic.

Feed according to your horse's individual requirements

Two horses of the same height, age and breed may require different diets. Factors to consider are: height, age, condition, breed, exercise regime, temperament, fitness and time of year.

Feed plenty of roughage

Roughage is a good source of fibre and bulks out the horse's diet. Sources of roughage include hay, haylage and chaffs.

Feed little and often

Horses are 'trickle feeders': their digestive tract is designed to cope with small amounts of food at regular intervals. Large meals twice daily can cause a horse to bolt its feed and could even lead to colic or choke. This will also overload the stomach, which would result in the undigested food being passed out in faeces.

Never make sudden changes to your horse's diet

The gut of a horse contains bacteria that adapt according to the foods passed through it; this adaptation needs to happen slowly over a period of time. Introduce a new feed gradually, increasing it over a period of time. This rule also applies to a new batch of hay or forage, especially if obtained from a different supplier.

Stick to a feeding routine

Horses expect their food to arrive at the same time each day. This anticipation of food may cause problems. Stabled horses may become agitated and bang on the doors; fights may occur among turned-out horses gathering at the gate at feed times. Altering their feeding regimes may also cause digestive upsets.

Always feed succulents

Ideally, horses should have access to grass every day, but this is not always possible. Succulents provide an additional source of vitamins and minerals and can help stimulate appetites.

Never exercise your horse immediately after feeding

On average it takes a horse one-and- a-half hours to process food through the stomach into the small intestine. Digestion can be interrupted if the horse is asked to exercise. A horse should be fed well in advance of being exercised, or afterwards.

Provide a constant fresh water supply

Water aids the digestion process; helps produce saliva; and acts as a lubricant when food is passing through the digestive tract.

Always practise good hygiene

- Buckets, scoops and spoons should be scrubbed clean.
- Feed room floors should be kept scrupulously clean.
- Feed should always be kept in rodent-free bins.
- Empty feed bins should be washed out and throroughly dried.
- Forage should be kept in a clean, dry, well-ventilated store.

Always measure out quantities of hay/feed

Weighing food avoids over- or under- feeding. Weigh an empty scoop, then add each different food, and weigh the scoop again. Subtract the weight of the empty scoop from the total weight when the feed is added. Measure hay/forage with a weigh hook.

Feed compositions

Horse feed can be divided up into five main groups: protein, carbohydrates, fibre, vitamins and minerals, and lipids – fats and oils. They all have a function in a horse's diet.

You can feed hay and haylage to your horse in a net to prevent wastage.

Protein

This is essential for growth and repair. It is formed from chains of amino acids; the horse produces some amino acids, while others are produced in the gut by micro-organisms. However, not all essential amino acids are produced naturally by the horse and therefore these need to be included in its diet.

Carbohydrates

These are a horse's main source of energy. They include:
• Cellulose: this is insoluble carbohydrate (also known as fibre).
• Sugars: these are carbohydrates in their simplest form.
• Starch: this is the plant's major energy store.

Fibre

Without fibre, your horse would find it difficult to digest his food. It stimulates the gut to contract, which allows for the passage of food. The majority of a horse's diet should contain fibre. It can be found in forage, including hay, straw and grass.

Vitamins and minerals

Vitamins can be divided into two groups: water soluble and fat soluble. Water-soluble vitamins cannot be stored in the body unlike fat-soluble ones. If a horse is fed a correctly balanced diet and has a normal work regime, it is unlikely to need supplemented vitamins. Each vitamin plays a part in maintaining equine health. Minerals, like vitamins, are only required in small quantities, and supplements are rarely needed if a horse is fed a nutritious diet.

Feed types

These can be categorized as follows: roughage (grass, hay, silage, haylage, processed feeds, straw and chaffs); concentrates (compounds and cereals); supplements (vitamins and minerals); and succulents, including carrots, apples and swedes.

Roughage

This is a very important food group for all horses and ponies, and it includes the following items.

Grass

Horses and ponies have evolved to survive on grass. Quality (i.e. its nutritional value) and quantity will vary greatly between pastures. The majority of horses' diets consist purely of grass from spring through to autumn, with many on restricted grazing to prevent problems, such as laminitis and obesity. You must monitor your horse's body condition on a daily basis if he lives out at grass. In the winter, when grass may be sparse, supplemented hay or feed may be required to maintain a good body condition.

Hay

When producing hay, cutting must be performed in the right weather conditions and at the correct time of year, so that the best quality hay is produced. Different grasses are used in haymaking, each having its own nutritional values. Hay should be kept in a cool, dry, well-ventilated store. Good-quality hay is dust free, pleasant smelling, and free from mould, damp, thistles and weeds. Note that ragwort in hay is poisonous and should never be fed to horses (see page 69).

Feeding your horse freshly cut and baled hay can be harmful because it is still developing; ingestion of this hay can even cause digestive upsets, such as colic, laminitis and metabolic

If feeding haylage or hay from a net, make sure you know the weight. Giving a smaller net three times a day will help to keep a stabled horse occupied.

disorders. Therefore do not feed new hay until about three months post baling. Like any new food, you should always be sure to introduce it gradually.

Silage

This less matured crop of grass has a much higher nutritional value than haylage and hay, and a high level of additives, but care must be taken if it is given to horses because if it is not fed correctly it can predispose them to botulism, resulting in colic, obesity, laminitis and other metabolic and digestive upsets.

Haylage

Available in vacuum-packed, sealed plastic wrapping, good-quality haylage has a high nutritional value and is free from dust. It should not be fed within the first two months post cutting. Haylage is similar to silage, except that it is wilted for longer, allowing the extraction of air. It must be stored carefully without puncturing the bags. If it is home produced, have its nutritional value analyzed before it is fed, so that this can be accounted for when devising your feeding rations and regimes.

Pelleted or dried grasses

Cut at different intervals in the season, concentrated grass products are high in carbohydrates and protein. They are usually classed as part of the concentrate, not the roughage, ration.

Straw

Oat or barley straw can be fed as a bulk food and is comparable to poor-quality hay. Straw is usually fed to horses on a controlled diet in order to add bulk to their daily ration.

Chaff/chop

Chaff or chop is made up of chopped straw and hay and sold in feed sacks. It can be bought mixed with molasses, honey and/or

All stabled horses should be turned out every day for a few hours to graze. In the wild, the horse's diet will consist mainly of grasses.

flavoured with apple, etc. It is useful for stabled horses, those on restricted diets, and horses that rush their food. These products are high in fibre and are usually fed to provide bulk in the diet.

Concentrates

These are divided into straight feeds (not mixed) and compound feeds. Cereals are straight feeds and include oats, barley, wheat, rice and maize. A good source of carbohydrates, they contain a sufficient level of protein, but lack calcium. Cereal grains can increase horses' excitability and/or energy levels.

Oats

These provide a good source of carbohydrates as well as starch, protein and fibre. It is essential that the oats used are of top quality in order to ensure maximum utilization by the horse. As they do not have a high calcium to phosphorus ratio, supplements are required to balance this out, especially for young horses. They are not advisable for horses that are worked lightly or irregularly.

Barley

This should never be fed unless it has been processed for horses. Its energy content is higher than that of oats, but the fibre content is lower. It has a low calcium to phosphorus ratio and supplementation may be required. Flaked barley is easier for horses to digest, although this is a more expensive product.

Maize

Maize is usually fed cooked or flaked. The digestible energy is higher than in oats, but the fibre content is lower. Maize is high in starch and can cause digestive problems if fed in excess.

Wheat

Wheat should never be fed as a whole as it can cause digestive problems. It is not commonly used as a feed for horses.

Processing
Cereal foods are processed using the following methods:
- Bruising
- Steam pelleting
- Steam flaking
- Extruding
- Micronizing

Bran

You should be aware that this is a by-product with a poor nutritional value; if fed in large quantities it can act as a laxative; it is high in fibre but low in protein; it is difficult to digest and has a bad calcium to phosphorus ratio.

Linseed

Cook this before feeding to soften it and inactivate the poisonous hydrocyanic acid, which is present in the seeds. Weigh it before cooking as no more than 100 g (3$^1/_2$ oz) should be fed in a horse's daily ration. Linseed is usually fed because it is a good energy source and improves coat condition.

Sugar beet

This is available as shredded pulp or cubes, and must be soaked before feeding. It is a good energy provider, easily digestible, a source of digestible fibre, and releases glucose slowly. Rich in calcium, salt and potassium, it can be used as a balancer to add to cereal feeds which are lacking in these nutrients. It is also useful for adding to dried food and 'bulking' up a horse's rations. It encourages the horse to eat more slowly, masticate the hard feed more effectively, and can sometimes act as an appetizer.

Compounds

These may be cubes or coarse mixes. Cubes are ground up, steamed and then pelleted. They come in a range of types for different horses. Coarse mixes range from high-protein mixes to a basic plain cereal mix. The contents may be flaked, micronized or rolled. To make them more palatable, syrup or molasses are sometimes added. Check the label to see whether vitamins and minerals are included, which reduces the need for supplements. To encourage your horse to eat more slowly and chew food properly, it is advisable to add some form of bulk to his compound feed or grain. Sugar beet or a form of chaff is often favoured for this.

Succulents

These include cut grass, some fresh vegetables, herbs, plants and fruit, and seaweed. Cut grass is safe for horses, provided it is long, fed immediately after being cut, and has been scythed. Lawn mowings should never be fed as they may cause severe colic. Carrots, apples, cabbage leaves and pea pods do no harm if fed in small quantities. Horses often select herbs from their grazing; they are usually high in essential minerals and trace elements. Garlic is fed as a powder or granules. It is helpful for treating respiratory problems, disguises the unpleasant taste of some medicines, and is as an effective fly repellent. Comfrey contains a high content of easily absorbed calcium, while dandelion leaves are high in vitamins and minerals. Nettles are a good source of iron and other minerals but must be cut and wilted before feeding. Seaweed is organic and high in iodine, and hence the amount you feed to your horse needs to be carefully monitored.

Supplements

If feeding a compound food, you must check which supplements are added; additional supplements are often not needed. Supplements can be detrimental if fed in excess. If a mixture of straight feeds is fed, check the rations and nutritional values, as they may be low in calcium, salt, lysine and methionine. Do not consider vitamins and minerals individually, as they can interact with each other. Seek expert advice and guidance when adding these to a horse's diet. Supplements include salt, dried herbs, vitamins, minerals (including trace elements), feed balancers, and bacterial cultures.

Feed balancers and salt

Feed balancers come in small cubes, which are a good source of vitamins, minerals, some probotics and protein. They are designed to be added to a horse's daily ration of food. Monitor how much salt your horse has by adding it to the daily feed. You can place a rock of salt in his manger to help prevent him bolting his food, or provide a salt lick in the stable or a salt block in his field.

Preparing food

The way in which food is fed to the horse is an important factor which is often not taken into consideration when owners are devising feeding regimes. Horse feeds are expensive and they should be stored and prepared correctly in order to prevent wastage and to allow maximum utilization.

Mould spores

Some horses are allergic mould spores in chaffs, hay and straw. Horses and ponies bedded on mouldy material are at risk of inhaling more spores than their respiratory system can manage. The spores will eventually reach the bottom of the airways, and although a healthy animal should be able to recover, in an allergy-prone horse a disease state is stimulated. Allergic horses should be fed soaked hay to prevent the spores entering their airways.

Feeding hay

There are a number of ways in which hay can be fed to a horse. These include the following methods:

Hay mangers

These are less wasteful than feeding hay loose on the ground. However, they are not a good idea as they can be difficult to clean, and it is easy for a horse to pull the contents out on to the floor. Also, the hay spores are trapped and horses can breathe them in easily.

Loose on the ground

This imitates the way a horse would eat in the wild. It also saves you time, is less labour intensive than filling a haynet (see opposite), and is safer for the horse as no haynets or racks are used. However, this method does have some disadvantages. It can become untidy and wasteful as the hay could be trampled into bedding or the ground. The horse may urinate and/or defecate on it. It may be difficult and awkward to present soaked hay to the horse in this manner, and it is harder to weigh. The hay should be shaken before feeding and weighed by placing the loose hay in a sack. This makes transporting the hay across the yard less wasteful and keeps the yard tidy.

Haynets

These prevent wastage and make it easier to weigh and soak hay. Small-holed nets encourage horses to eat more slowly, thus helping prevent boredom. The net must be tied up correctly (see below) and high enough to prevent a horse trapping a leg or it falling down when tugged. Hay should be shaken, placed in a haynet and weighed. Bear in mind that once the hay has been eaten, the net will hang lower to the ground than it did when full. Hence it should be tied as high as possible and secured with a quick-release knot.

Tying up a haynet

1 Start off by putting the string through the haynet ring on the stable wall.

2 Next, pull the haynet up as high as possible to touch the ring.

3 Put the string through the bottom of the net. Pull it as tight as possible.

4 Use a quick-release knot round the string to make the haynet firm.

5 Now put the end of the string through the quick-release safety knot.

6 Lastly, you must turn the knot towards the wall of the box.

Soaking hay

This is fed to horses with an allergic cough. Weigh the hay, then place in a haynet and soak in water for up to 10 minutes. Hang it up to drip dry, but not dry out completely, before feeding. Hay should never be soaked for longer than 30 minutes, as valuable soluble nutrients will be lost to the water.

In a hayrack

Hayracks tend to be attached high up on a wall. There is the possibility of hayseeds entering the horse's eyes, so they should always be placed at an appropriate height. A hayrack can also be a potential hazard in a box.

Soaking sugar beet

Sugar beet must *always* be soaked in cold water before feeding to your horse. Whereas the cubes require 24 hours' soaking, shredded pulp needs only 12 hours. You need enough water to make the sugar beet soft but not too watery. If they are not adequately soaked, the cubes or shreds could swell in the horse's stomach and could even cause an impaction and/or colic and choking.

In hot weather, sugar beet should always be kept in a cool place, as heat will cause it to ferment. Fermentation will also occur if the sugar beet is left soaked for too long, and hence a new supply should be soaked each day.

Mashes

Bran mashes are the most traditional form but they appear to have few benefits. They were once fed to horses after a strenuous day's exercise or rest day, but they are now considered problematic, as they are not a balanced food. Occasionally feeding bran mashes means sudden changes are made to a horse's diet, and thus the food is not utilized and digested properly.

● A bran mash usually takes about 20 minutes to prepare. Boiling water is poured onto the bran until the texture is of crumbly but not wet. The mash should then be covered and set aside until it is cool enough to feed to the horse.

• A linseed mash is prepared in exactly the same way, except that the water from cooked linseed is used instead of boiling water.

• Barley mash is prepared in the same manner as a bran mash, except the boiling water is poured on to the flaked barley or, as an alternative, cooked barley can be fed when cooled.

Cooking barley or oats

Barley or oats can be boiled in a large pan. Careful monitoring of the water needs to be taken into consideration as not enough can lead to evaporation, a burnt pan and spoilt feed, while too much can cause loss of goodness. Whole barley needs between three and four hours of steady simmering, whereas oats take about one-and-a-half to two hours, as their husks are softer. Check they are cooked properly by pressing the grain between finger and thumb: they should feel soft and most of the water should have been absorbed.

Cooking linseed

It is important to destroy the enzyme linase before the linseed has time to release hydrocyanic acid. You can do this by placing the linseed in boiling water. Make sure that enough water is used, as, when cooled, the linseed will turn to jelly. Once the water has come to a boil, reduce the heat and then simmer gently for four to six hours. The cooked seeds and jelly are added to the feed when they have cooled down, or they can be added warm as a liquid to make a linseed mash.

When you are feeding your horse a carrot, you should always cut it in half lengthways in order to avoid the hazard of choking.

Oatmeal gruel
Approximately two handfuls of oatmeal should be placed in a bucket. Add boiling water while stirring, then leave to cool before feeding.

Storage and hygiene

It is vitally important to ensure that you are scrupulous at all times about cleanliness and stable hygiene. Many horses are very fussy about their food and they can be put off easily, so don't give them an excuse with poor hygiene.

Storage

When you are planning and organizing your feed room, it is very important to think carefully about how you will store the feed as well as some basic hygiene considerations. All types of feed can deteriorate if they are stored in poor conditions.

Ideally, feed should be stored at a low temperature; where there is minimal or no temperature variation; in an environement with low humidity and good ventilation; and in a closed container which is out of direct sunlight.

It should also be protected from infestation by rats, mice, birds, insects and mites. A good-quality metal bin or a plastic dustbin will prove cost-effective in the long run by reducing the amount of food that is wasted from being kept in poor conditions.

Storing vacuum-packed forage
It is important that vacuum-packed bags are not punctured, as they must stay airtight until they are to be used. Vacuum-packed forage must be kept safely away from rodents, which may chew the plastic, as well as from sunlight, and any sharp edges that may puncture the bags.

Storing hay
All hay will deteriorate over a period of time, but the provision of good storage conditions will keep it edible for a longer period. It is important to protect hay from the weather, especially damp, to provide good ventilation, and keep it vermin-proof.

Water

Water plays an essential role in all the horse's bodily functions. Although a horse could survive for weeks without food, it would probably die after about six days of having no water. So it is essential that your horse has constant access to water.

Water purity and systems

Make sure the water provided is always clean and fresh. If it is contaminated, the horse may reject it. Cover the water-storage tank to protect it from dust particles and vermin. If your horse is choosy about what he drinks or if he plays with the water, it may be a sign that it is contaminated.

Automatic water bowls provide a constant water supply, but it is quite difficult to monitor how much the horse is drinking. They can also be hard to clean and may freeze in cold weather. They should always be large enough for horses to place their muzzles in them.

Buckets enable easy monitoring of how much water is drunk by a horse, but they do not provide a constant supply. They can be easily knocked over and are labour intensive. They should be sited in a corner well away from the stable door, placed in a rubber tyre for stability. Make sure you clean them twice a day and top them up regularly with fresh, clean water.

Horses living out at grass should always have access to a clean, fresh supply of water.

Dehydration

This is when a horse does not have enough fluid in its body to sustain normal physiological conditions. This occurs when more salts and water are lost from the horse's body than are taken in. Causes include fast, energetic work; sweating; heat exhaustion; urinating excessively; diarrhoea; haemorrhage; and lack of available water. Dehydration can cause death in the most severe cases but can also lead to serious health problems.

Planning a special diet

Like humans, horses come in differing shapes and sizes, and their energy expenditure and workloads will vary. In order to maintain good condition and a fit and healthy lifestyle, each individual horse's needs must be taken into consideration.

Temperament
It is often difficult to feed excitable horses enough hard food for the work they carry out without increasing their excitability. These horses often tend to be better on plenty of roughage and a feed that does not contain too much cereal.

If your horse lives out and the grass is of good quality, he may not need any additional feed in the spring and summer months.

Devising a feeding regime

Depending on the horse's size, age, type and the time of year, work out a maintenance ration – how much food is needed to keep a horse that is not in work in good condition. Next work out how much energy ration the horse will need, whether it's for work or growth. Decide what concentrates to feed, taking into account their energy and protein value.

Size, type, age and condition

Native-type horses and ponies tend to require less hard food than warmblooded types. Young, growing horses that are in work may need hard food for extra carbohydrates and protein which are utilized during exercise. Old horses may need extra rations in cold weather as well as easily digestible and masticated food. Condition scoring (see page 159) is essential for assessing the overall condition of the horse and to assist in devising a suitable diet.

Height and weight

A horse's height and weight provide a guide to feeding him, although this is not an accurate method of determining the correct regime. The easiest way of estimating a horse's weight is to use a specially calculated equine weigh tape, available at most feed stores and tack shops. Weigh bridges are the most accurate method for weighing horses.

Weather

As food is used to maintain the body temperature of a horse, weather conditions must be considered when planning a feed ration. If it is cold, horses will need more food to help maintain the extra heat. It is the risk of losing body fat in cold weather that makes winter feeding very important for most horses.

Economy and availability

Feeding cheap, poor-quality food is a false economy as it is harder to keep a horse in good condition. When possible, enough forage, such as hay, should be bought and stored, as it can be in short supply in late winter.

Work and circumstances

Provided that grass is of good quality and quantity, horses living out without doing any work should need no additional feed. In spring and summer, grass is usually of high nutritional value, but horses may need restricted grazing. During the winter, the grass is of lower nutritional value, and horses living out, without doing any work, may need supplementary food to keep their condition. Monitor their weight carefully: long winter coats and rugs often hide sticking-out ribs. If your horse is regularly exercised strenuously, do not over-feed him in an attempt to create fitness. If he is not going to do strenuous work, feed a compound feed, in the form of a mix or cubes to ensure that all the required vitamins and minerals he needs are included in the one feed. The majority of his diet should consist of roughage.

want to know more?
- Ask your vet for advice on special diets, or if your horse is allergic to the spores in hay and straw
- For equine weigh tapes, contact your local feed store or tack shop
- Check if your local livery yard or veterinary practice has a weigh bridge to weigh horses
- Leaflets are available from the BHS on basic feeding and diet

weblinks
- Visit the BHS website at: www.bhs.org.uk
- Online information service for horse owners available at the Horse and Hound website at: www.horseandhound.co.uk

7 The healthy horse

The way in which you keep your horse and how you care for him will affect his general health and wellbeing. Practising preventive medicine with good general management, parasite control, regular foot trimming and shoeing, dentistry, a good diet and routine vaccinations will help to keep your horse healthy. However, if he seems unwell, you must identify the cause and ensure he receives the necessary care and treatment to restore him to good health. If he is ill or in pain, contact your vet immediately. Delay may prolong a health problem or even, in some cases, make the condition worse.

Observing a horse

Regular observation of all the horses under your care is crucial. It is obvious when a horse is seriously sick, but do you know whether your horse is feeling 100 per cent? The more you know what a horse is usually like, the easier it is to spot a problem.

To take a horse's temperature, just move the tail aside and then gently insert a lubricated thermometer into the anus at an angle so it presses against the rectal wall.

Think ABC

A simple way of remembering what to look for in your horse is to think ABC: Appearance, Behaviour and Condition. Check each one in turn. A responsible owner should also know their horse's normal vital signs: temperature, pulse and respiratory rate (TPR).

- T: the normal temperature is 37.5–38.5°C (99–101.5°F).
- P: the normal pulse is 36–42 beats per minute.
- R: the normal respiratory rate at rest is 8–14 breaths per minute.

Taking the temperature

An easy-to-read digital thermometer is ideal. If you use a glass thermometer, shake the mercury down to the end first. Grease the measuring end of the thermometer with petroleum jelly. With someone steadying the horse's head and reassuring it, stand to one side of the rear, run your hand over the quarters and grasp the base of the tail firmly. Gently lift it and insert the thermometer through the anus. Hold the tail so the horse does not clamp it down, and hang onto the thermometer. Stay to the side to avoid being kicked. Insert the thermometer for a minute, tilting it against the rectum wall. Remove gently, wipe clean and read it. Afterwards, clean it with cold water and disinfectant.

Increased or low temperature

A slightly increased temperature is not usually serious, and quite normal after exercise. But a high temperature – much more than 39.5°C (102.5°F) – is potentially serious. It suggests the horse is

unwell: you should contact your veterinary surgeon for advice.
A very low temperature also indicates that the horse could be
unwell and may be shocked. Check with your vet.

Measuring the pulse

The best place to feel a horse's pulse is where the facial artery
passes under the jaw. Make sure that the horse's head is still and
that he is not eating when you do this. The horse's resting pulse
is slow, so it can be difficult to detect. You can practise finding
your horse's pulse after exercise, when it is more obvious.

Finding the pulse

Run your fingers along the inside of the bony lower edge of the
jaw. The pulsing artery will be felt as a tubular structure. If you
lightly press this against the jaw with the flat of your first three
fingers, you will feel the pulse. Count the number of beats in
15 seconds and multiply by four to get the pulse rate per minute.
Bear in mind that the pulse rate will increase with exercise,
excitement, a high temperature or pain. If you cannot feel the
pulse, feel for the heartbeat between the ribs on the left side of
the lower chest, just behind the elbow in the girth area.

Respiratory rate

To check this, you can either hold a hand close to the horse's
nostrils to feel each breath or count the flank movements.
On a cold day, you will be able to see when the horse exhales.
appearance to assess his level of health.

Eyes and gums

The mucous membranes around the eyes and on the gums
should be a healthy pink colour, apart from the occasional horse
with dark pigmented gums. With serious illness, the membranes
change colour. You can check the circulation by measuring the
'capillary refill time'. Firmly press a pink area of the horse's gums

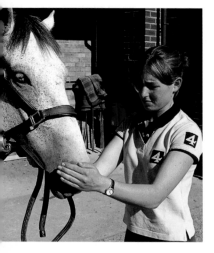

To measure a horse's respiratory rate, hold your hand close to his nostrils and feel each breath. On a cold day, you will be able to see easily when he exhales.

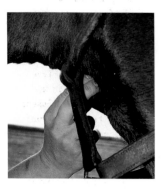

To take a horse's pulse, which is normally 36 to 42 per minute, place your first three fingers under the back of the lower jawbone. You will feel the artery pulsating beneath the skin just on the inside of the jaw, but it requires practice.

with your fingertip. Initially this should be pale (blanched), but the normal colour should return within three seconds. A delay may suggest a circulatory problem, such as shock. Sweating for no obvious reason implies that something is wrong and is sometimes a sign of pain.

Mental state

A horse's mental state is yet another relatively reliable indicator of how healthy he is. If your horse appears to be unusually dull or excited, then maybe something is wrong with him.

Lameness

Although it will be obvious when a horse is very lame, milder lameness can be quite difficult to assess. If you are unsure whether your horse is lame, you should ask someone to trot him away from you in a straight line and then back towards you, with the horse's head held loosely, so you can watch it move.

Front- or hind-limb lameness

A horse that is lame in the front legs will lift its head up as the lame leg hits the ground. Its head nods down as the sound leg hits the ground. Hind-limb lameness is easiest to observe as the horse is trotted away from you. The hip on the painful lame side will appear to rise and fall more obviously as the horse tries to avoid taking any weight on that leg.

Severe lameness

If a horse is severely lame it is unwise to trot it up. If it lies down more than normal it may be due to severe lameness, often in more than one foot, e.g. laminitis.

What goes in

Ponies are almost always hungry, and therefore if they stop eating it usually means that something is wrong. Horses tend to be fussier and will stop eating if they are excited or disturbed. Very fit animals can be surprisingly 'picky' eaters.

You should know what your individual horse's appetite is like. For many, being off their food is the most obvious clue that they are unwell.

Horses drink about 20–45 litres (4–9 gallons) of water a day, but this will vary according to the individual, the weather conditions, their work load and also the moisture content of their diet. Dehydration has to be severe before it is obvious; if your horse is not drinking, then it is important to double-check everything else.

What comes out

Loose droppings or diarrhoea should always be a cause for concern for every horse owner. You should also be concerned if your horse passes fewer droppings than normal as this may be a sign of constipation or even impending colic.

Urine should also be checked. It is normal for a horse's urine to be a cloudy yellow colour, but it varies from a pale yellow to brown. If you notice that there is a change in the usual colour, and particularly if it appears red, be concerned. Similarly, if a horse is repeatedly straining to pass urine, it suggests that there is pain somewhere.

In all these instances, you should consult your vet without delay and get some expert advice. Do not adopt a wait and see policy; it is better to check it out and be safe rather than sorry.

Digital pulse
If a foot problem is present, a stronger than normal digital pulse may be felt where the digital artery runs over the sides of the fetlock. Compare the different feet. If there is a foot abscess developing, the pulse will be stronger and easier to find. If you find a pounding digital pulse in more than one foot, the most likely cause is laminitis.

Body condition

This is an important reflection of a horse's diet, exercise and general state of health. By monitoring the body condition of your horse, you can discover a lot about his physical state.

Underweight

Common reasons for a horse to be in poor condition and under-weight are: insufficient feed or grazing, and inadequate care, possibly associated with parasite infestation, dental disease, inadequate shelter in cold wet weather, or even bullying by other horses which can prevent a horse eating enough.

Overweight

Many horses, particularly ponies, are 'good doers', gaining weight easily, particularly as many are given too much feed and too little exercise. There is a higher risk of laminitis and other serious lameness in overweight animals. Native ponies are most at risk, since naturally they inhabit mountains and moorlands, yet they are often kept on lush lowland grazing. Spring and autumn are the critical times of year for fatties because the new grass is too rich for them. Any overweight animal should not be turned out at grass, as they will only get fatter. Laminitis is most common in ponies turned out on lush spring grass, but it is also seen in horses that have had too much feed.

Condition scoring

This is used to assess a horse's physical state. There are a variety of scoring systems but they all work on the principle of assessing fat deposits. It is important to rely on feeling areas such as over the ribs, as a shaggy winter coat or rugs may disguise thinness. You should be able to feel but not see a horse's ribs, although there are better systems (see the table opposite).

Condition scoring

To obtain the condition score for any horse or pony, first score the pelvis, then adjust the pelvis score up or down by 0.5 if it differs by one or more points from the back or neck score.

Score	Condition	Pelvis	Back and ribs	Neck
0	Very poor	Angular, skin tight; very sunken rump; deep cavity under tail	Skin tight over ribs; very prominent and sharp backbone	Marked ewe neck; narrow and slack at base
1	Poor	Prominent pelvis and croup; sunken rump but skin supple; deep cavity under tail	Ribs easily visible; prominent backbone with skin sunken on either side	Ewe neck; narrow and slack at base
2	Moderate	Rump flat either side of backbone; croup well defined, some fat; slight cavity under tail	Ribs just visible; back-bone covered but spine can be felt	Narrow but firm
3	Good	Covered by fat and rounded; no gutter; pelvis easily felt	Ribs just covered and easily felt; no gutter along back; backbone well covered but spine can be felt	No crest (except for stallions), firm neck
4	Fat	Gutter to root of tail; pelvis covered by soft fat; need firm pressure to feel	Ribs well covered; need pressure to feel	Slight crest; wide and firm
5	Very fat	Deep gutter to root of tail; skin distended; pelvis buried and cannot be felt	Ribs buried; cannot be felt; deep gutter along back; back broad and flat	Marked crest; very wide and firm; fold of fat

Weight loss tips

• Ask your vet for advice to ensure your horse really needs to lose weight and to devise a programme of diet and exercise.

• Weight reduction should be slow and steady so as not to stress the horse or create any metabolic disturbance. Don't rush it.

• Make gradual changes in the type and amount of feed given to a horse. Unless recommended otherwise by your vet, reduce the rations by no more than 10 per cent over a seven-to-ten-day period.

• Monitor your horse's progress by using a weigh tape or just a long piece of string to measure the reduction in the girth. However,

Maintaining condition

If you do manage to slim your horse down to its ideal body condition, it is important to maintain it, and this means carefully readjusting its rations to stabilize its weight. Exercise will continue to be important for weight maintenance, and you should never forget the fattening effect of grass; just think of it as being like chocolate for the human weight watcher.

remember that a weigh tape will only provide an approximation. When the weight plateaus, you can gradually cut back the ration again.

• Gradually up the time and intensity of exercise as your horse's fitness improves. Never feed him more in anticipation of increased work.

• Provide plenty of fresh water, even though the food intake is reduced. This can help the horse's digestive and other systems to function efficiently.

• Use forage feeds with plenty of high-quality fibre which are low in total energy, e.g. switch from alfalfa to meadow hay. Hay that is made from older plants, i.e. late cut, has an increased fibre content, a lower percentage of leaves and likely to be less fattening.

• Measure feed by weight, not by volume (scoops or buckets) to determine the appropriate rations.

• A horse is naturally a grazing animal which spends a lot of time nibbling. Maximize the time taken to eat a given amount by using double or treble haynets to reduce the amount pulled out with each bite. When seriously restricting feed intake, e.g. with a laminitic, your vet may suggest scattering hay in among non-edible bedding, so the horse has to hunt for it.

• Feed the overweight horse separately from others, so it cannot steal any other horse's feed.

• Never feed more than is needed for a horse's level of work. An overweight animal can have a forage-based diet, i.e. grass and/or hay. For many horses doing a small amount of work per day, this is enough except in winter. Any extra hard food should not give your horse too much energy. Your vet will advise which one is best for your horse.

• You could consider soaking the hay for fat ponies, in order to leach out soluble carbohydrates.

Preventing problems

You can prevent a wide range of common health problems in horses by putting some simple measures into practice. These include worm control, foot and dental care, and vaccination.

Worm control

Effective worm control is important because internal parasitic infestation with different equine worms produces many health problems, ranging from loss of appetite, reduced performance, loss of weight and poor coat condition to potentially fatal conditions, such as colic or diarrhoea. The main factors leading to infection are as follows:

• High stocking density

• Over-grazed pasture, so that horses are forced to graze close to piles of droppings and eat grass close to the ground where larvae live.

• Use of the same fields by mixed age groups of horses, especially young horses, which are more likely to be heavily infected with worms.

• The presence of any horses with high worm egg counts – they are significantly infected and will infect other horses and ponies.

• Warm damp weather, such as is common in the United Kingdom.

Designing a programme

A variety of effective parasite control measures are available to protect your horse, even if there are no apparent signs of worms. General guidelines are available, often from wormer manufacturers. However, such information is no substitute for an

Carrying out effective pasture management will help to control worms. Tests on blood and the droppings are useful to see if any treatment is needed.

Beware
If you are administering a wormer treatment, ensure your horse eats it immediately. There have been instances of dogs being poisoned by eating leftover wormer powders or paste. The treatment itself is less effective if left in the feed.

individually designed worm control programme to fit your horse's particular circumstances available from your veterinary surgeon, who will advise you on the following issues.

Pasture hygiene

The daily removal of droppings is a highly effective means of controlling the spread of worms between horses. It is tedious but effective. Keeping your horses off the fields allows infective eggs and larvae on 'resting' paddocks to die before they can infect another horse. Depending on the weather conditions, this can take a long time – a minimum rest period of six months. However, in warm weather a year or more may be needed – so it is rarely practical.

Mixed species grazing is helpful. Cattle and sheep act as 'biological vacuum cleaners', eating the eggs and larvae, which cannot survive in species other than the horse. Do not over-stock pasture, otherwise horses will graze closer to dung piles and any worm-infected grass. Harrowing of the pastures is not ideal as it merely spreads parasites around the paddocks.

Using worming medication

Different worming treatments will eliminate different parasites. Your vet will advise what is most appropriate. Read medication instructions carefully and ensure you know what compound you are giving: there are various brand named products, which have the same key ingredients. Follow the instructions, so they are not used more frequently than recommended and the correct dose is given for the size of horse.

Diagnostic testing

This is a very cost-effective way of determining whether your horses actually require treating for worms. Diagnostic testing can also be used once or twice a year to check worm control programmes are working.

A common way of worming a horse is to use a special worming syringe. Hold the horse's head with one hand and then squirt the contents into the animal's mouth.

A faecal worm egg count simply requires you to submit a small (teaspoon-sized), labelled sample of fresh droppings to your vet or lab for analysis. This will assess the number of worm eggs present, which is useful for checking the parasite status of a particular horse and deciding whether or not it needs treatment. A result of less than 200 eggs per gram is acceptable and usually indicates that treatment for worms is not required. A blood sample can be taken and sent for a specific antibody test for tapeworms. Routine worm egg counts do not detect tapeworms, so blood tests are useful to screen healthy horses as well as those with recurrent colic.

Failure of worm control

- Drug resistance is developing, so some wormers may no longer be effective. Check with your veterinary surgeon.
- Lack of synchronization of dosing within an entire group. This is a common problem in big livery yards, where there is no co-ordinated control programme and the untreated horses may re-infect the treated animals. Check the yard's policy if your horse is at livery.
- Underdosing due to underestimating the horse's body weight.
- Introducing new animals into the grazing without treating them.
- Extending the interval between doses beyond the period of activity of the various wormers.
- Using the wrong treatment; for instance, only certain wormers (containing pyrantel or praziquantel) are effective against tapeworms.
- Drug treatment will not destroy all the immature or larval worms. A particular problem is some forms of cyathostomes (small red worms) encyst or bury themselves inside the equine gut wall, where they are relatively inaccessible to treatment. They will then hatch out at a later date and will cause problems, particularly severe diarrhoea, if many such worms emerge at once.

Foot care

Hooves should be checked, trimmed and, if shod, shoes should be regularly renewed by a registered farrier. To avoid lameness, check your horse's feet. Good foot shape or conformation plays a critical role because of its relationship to the way in which the foot is a working part of the horse's body as it moves.

An unshod hoof, clearly showing the internal structure with the sole and the sensitive frog (plantar cushion) both visible.

Being well shod

You and your farrier should be doing everything to maintain your horse's feet in the best possible condition. The Farriers Registration Council maintains a register of farriers (see page 188), but personal recommendation is best. Farriers frequently say correctly that they are not consulted often enough. Mostly, a horse's feet need attention every four to six weeks. Regular trimming and shoeing are essential to keep the feet in good shape. After six weeks, the shoe may not be falling off but the toe will be getting long, so the horse is more likely to stumble.

Signs of foot problems

There are tell-tale signs of potential foot problems which are relatively easy to recognise in your horse.

A low heel/long toe shape

Often found in the Thoroughbred type of horse, this shape results in collapsed heels and extra pressure on the back of the foot, especially the navicular bone and surrounding soft tissue structures. It will increase the chance of heel pain developing, so avoid this. Frequently the heels will gradually collapse as the balance of the foot deteriorates.

Once a horse has collapsed heels, it is a difficult and lengthy procedure to correct them. It can take nearly a year for the hoof to grow down from the coronary band to the ground.

Sheared heels
There is a disparity between the medial and lateral heel heights of more than half a centimetre, i.e. the side to side balance is wrong.

Small feet and narrow heels
If feet are small and heels are narrow in relation to the size of the horse, there will be too much weight on too small a surface area.

Structure of the hoof
The horse's hoof forms an insensitive covering for the internal parts of the foot. It consists of the wall, sole and frog. The wall is the external part of the hoof when the foot is on the ground. It is thicker at the toe than at the heels, and grows from the coronary band, taking nine to twelve months before coming into wear at the toe; six months at the heel.

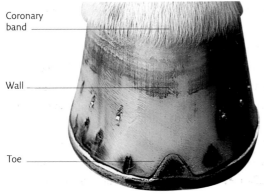

Coronary band

Wall

Toe

A front view of the hoof showing the the coronary band, a strip extending around the coronet and from which the hoof grows.

Dental care

Your horse's teeth should be examined at least once every six to twelve months. This will assist with comfortable riding for the competition horse and it will also aid early detection of any dental problems, particularly in older horses.

Always ensure that your vet or a qualified dental technician cares for your horse's teeth.

Dental checks

It is important to use vets and qualified equine dental technicians (EDTs) to care for your horse's teeth. You must always ensure that a competent qualified individual performs any dentistry.

Unlike humans, horses' teeth continually erupt or grow. The standard practice of feeding hay in a net or feed from a raised manger means they eat with their head up – an unnatural position for a horse designed to graze at ground level. This results in uneven tooth wear and the development of sharp hooks and points, which require removal, usually by rasping.

Signs of discomfort

By checking your horse on a daily basis, you will learn recognise any early warning signs of future dental problems and an uncomfortable mouth. Look for:
● Quidding – messy eating with partially chewed food being spilt as the horse eats.
● Slower eating or reluctance to eat.
● Tossing the head more than usual.
● Chewing or playing with the bit.
● A stiff-backed action, bucking or disobedience when schooling.

If you are in doubt, you should have your horse's mouth properly checked by the veterinary surgeon.

Contagious diseases

Currently in the United Kingdom there are a limited number of contagious equine diseases. However, with the increasing international travel of horses, there is an ever-present threat of the emergence of new or 'exotic' diseases.

Major diseases

Respiratory infections are the most important contagious diseases that can infect horses. These include the influenza virus, equine herpes viruses and strangles. Different preventive strategies are used for combating them. Many measures can be taken to reduce the risk of infection of horses by infectious and contagious diseases. Precautions vary with the individual diseases and depend on factors such as the natural history of the disease, its means of spread and the horse's immunity.

Vaccination

For some infectious diseases, such as the influenza virus, the widespread use of vaccination has an important role to play in their prevention. A large percentage of the horse population needs to be vaccinated to prevent major outbreaks.

Vaccination may not eliminate the risk of infection in a horse completely but it reduces the spread and is a major component in the overall preventive strategy for the horse population. Suitable vaccines, correctly administered at the correct times, are vital. A small number of horses may demonstrate reactions to vaccines, but only rarely, and this is not a logical reason why vaccination should not be undertaken.

Vaccinations
There are five diseases of horses for which vaccinations are currently available in the UK. These are as listed overleaf:

Vaccinations currently available

Tetanus

Otherwise known as lockjaw, this is a serious (often fatal) disease caused by toxins produced when spores of the bacteria *Clostridium tetani* multiply within a wound. They produce paralyzing muscle spasms and death by respiratory arrest. Horses are especially susceptible to tetanus and should be vaccinated. Vaccination regimes vary but all involve a primary course of two injections four to six weeks apart, followed by boosters at intervals of two to three years. In situations where an unvaccinated horse sustains a wound, tetanus antitoxin can be given to provide emergency protection.

Equine influenza

Vaccination is compulsory for horses competing under the rules of the Jockey Club and most other sporting organizations. More frequent booster vaccinations may be indicated for high-risk horses, such as young racehorses.

Equine viral arteritis (EVA)

This can cause fever, infertility and illness. It is called 'pink eye' because of inflammation in and around the eyes. It is a problem in breeding horses, where stallions can become carriers of the infection.

Equine herpes virus

Vaccination is available. It has been shown to provide some immunity against infection by the respiratory and abortion forms of the infection. It is uncertain whether it protects against the neurological form.

Strangles

A new vaccine may be beneficial in areas where strangles is a problem. It is recommended that a whole yard is immunized; frequent boosters are needed. The vaccine is administered as a tiny pinprick into the upper lip.

Preventing ill health

You can take a wide range of practical measures to keep your horse fit and healthy and to help prevent ill health. These are all relatively easy to put into practice, need not cost a lot of money, and they will benefit your horse and may help to prolong his life.

Dust-free environment

All horses will benefit from being kept in a dust-free environment, as will the people who care for them. Foot associated lameness, coughs and respiratory disease are the commonest problems for many horses and a concern for owners. The respiratory ideal is to turn your horse out to pasture and, with decent rugs, many horses can happily live out all year round, grazing permitting.

However, for many performance horses this is not practical. Instead, it is important to keep the stable environment as dust free as possible by selecting dust-free bedding (see page 43) and using good-quality hay. Most respiratory disease in the horse is caused or made worse by inhaling a combination of dust, bacterial endotoxins (toxic substances produced by bacterial cell walls) and moulds or fungal spores. The most common source is mouldy hay or straw.

Good ventilation is vital, so keep the top stable door open at all times and install a vent with a baffle in the opposite wall to ensure a constant flow of fresh air. Keeping the dust levels low in a stable environment is important for human health, as it will reduce the chances of people developing dust-induced coughs and asthma.

Avoiding injury
Horses are especially prone to injury. All possible precautions should be taken by a responsible owner including the following:
• Turn your horse out in a safe environment, e.g. avoid barbed wire.
• Care with companions: a high-stocking density, limited grazing and introduction of new horses will increase the risk of injury.
• Maintain a safe, healthy environment in and around any stable yard.

When to call the vet

If a horse suffers a major injury, or is clearly in pain, it is obvious that you need a vet straightaway. Yet there are some apparently minor injuries, which would also benefit from urgent veterinary attention, such as some small puncture wounds.

Recognising an emergency

All vets in practice in the UK provide 24-hour emergency care for all animals under their care. However, it is unreasonable to ring your vet at midnight for a horse that has been ill for three days; it is also unfair to leave a sick horse if it requires urgent attention.

Experience helps in recognising what is a true crisis. The vet may resolve an apparent crisis with some simple first aid advice and reassurance. Vets are trained to ask the right questions but rely on the owner to provide accurate answers. The person who contacts the vet should be the one who knows most about the horse. There is nothing worse than discussing a potentially serious problem third hand. If you have not actually seen the horse yourself, you will find it hard to explain what is wrong. Make a basic assessment before consulting the vet.

If your horse is lying down and is unable to get up but trying to do so, call the vet immediately.

Key points to consider

Pain
How much pain is the horse in? What are the frequency and duration of the signs of pain? Common indications, such as sweating, refusal to eat, agitation or depression, mean that the horse may need to be seen by your vet.

Vital signs
Check the horse's vital signs. Can you take the horse's temperature? Can you measure the pulse and breathing rate? Have they altered from normal?

Signs of injury
What does a wound look like and where is it on the body? A significant wound in association with lameness warrants a discussion with your vet as it may mean damage to deeper structures or the presence of infection.

Change from normal
Has there been a significant change from a horse's normal routine? Abdominal pain (colic) may affect a horse suddenly changed to a different diet. Grass sickness affects young animals turned out on different grazing.

How many are affected?
Multiple animals getting sick at once should raise a red flag. Signs of illness could indicate infectious diseases or a toxin in the pasture, water, or feed.

Lameness
Is the horse lame and unable to stand on the affected limb? If you suspect the bone might be involved, because it is exposed, or the leg is misshapen or abnormally floppy, urgent attention is essential as the horse could have a broken limb. If a horse is only mildly lame, it may be safe to wait and see. Lame horses should never be worked until the cause has been determined.

First aid

Horse owners need to know how to use appropriate first aid for any minor injuries as well as recognizing real emergencies. It is always best to be prepared to avoid panic in a crisis.

Be prepared

This means that you must know how to contact your vet in the event of an emergency; know where or how you can obtain horse transport in a hurry; and keep a well-stocked first-aid kit available.

Bandages

There are now many new bandaging materials available, so ask your vet to advise on the best options for your requirements. There will be occasions when you will need to bandage your horse's legs. Bandaging can provide both protection and support for the horse whilst working, travelling, resting or recovering from an injury.

Regardless of the purpose, it is essential that proper leg bandaging techniques are used (see page 122). If they are applied incorrectly, bandages will not only fail to help but they will also cause discomfort, by restricting the blood flow and potentially damaging tendons and other tissue. It is better to leave a horse's legs unbandaged than to bandage them incorrectly. If you have never bandaged a horse's legs, ask a vet or an equine nurse to show you.

Three layers

A bandage should always have three layers which are as follows:
• The inside, which is a non-stick clean dressing, such as melonin® (or rondopad®), which is attached next to a wound. If there is no wound but you are just applying a protective or support bandage, this is unnecessary.
• The middle layer of the bandage, which is the crucial padding that protects injuries, absorbs discharges, controls swelling and prevents

bandage rubs. If this layer is skimped, then the horse will suffer.

• The outer wrapping is important as this holds the bandage in place and provides extra support.

Bandaging knees/hocks

With a knee bandage, it is important to avoid any pressure on the two prominent points at the back and inside of the knee. Similarly, the point at the back of the hock is vulnerable to pressure sores. It is best to apply a figure-of-eight bandage, avoiding pressure on these vulnerable areas.

Key bandaging rules

• Always start with clean, dry legs and bandages.

• Use a thickness of at least 2 cm ($^3/_4$ in) of soft, clean padding to protect the leg beneath the bandage. Apply some padding, so that it lies flat and wrinkle-free against the skin. Cotton wool fits well around the limb.

• Bandage front to back, outside to inside (counter clockwise on left legs, clockwise on right legs) using a spiral pattern and smooth uniform pressure, working down the leg and up again, overlapping the preceding layer by 50 per cent.

• Avoid applying bandages too tightly or too loosely. Tight bandages cause injury, and loose bandages slip and will not provide proper support. Equally, ensure they are attached firmly, so they cannot come undone; use sticky tape over adherent bandages.

• To prevent bedding or debris getting into the bandage, you can seal the openings with a loose layer of flexible adhesive bandage.

• Bandage limbs in pairs. A horse will favour the injured limb, putting more weight on the sound leg. By bandaging limbs in pairs, the undamaged leg is supported, hopefully minimizing further injury.

• Watch for swelling above the bandage, increased lameness, or if the horse begins to chew at the bandage. If worried, contact your vet.

Duct tape

Duct tape is extremely useful as an outside layer to hold everything in place and provide a seal. If a horse does not like bandaging, a star-shape of sticky tape can be made up easily and then stuck on.

Bandaging feet

Disposable babies' nappies make a very effective dressing for a horse's foot. Their absorptive capacity and also their waterproofing powers are really phenomenal. A size 3 or 4 will fit the average riding horse's foot instead of a baby's bottom. A poultice or other dressing can be inserted as an inside layer within the nappy. If extra padding is needed for a tender foot, an additional nappy can provide it.

Changing bandages

In summary, you should not overdo this. A support bandage should be changed at least once a day. Wound dressings should be changed in accordance with veterinary advice, but most can be left on for longer than a day. If it is clean and dry, a leg bandage may stay on for a few days, but most foot dressings will get wet and they will need daily replacement.

If you are in doubt, always ask your vet for advice. Every time that you put on a clean dressing, it is expensive, and your vet will be able to advise you how often it really needs doing.

Tetanus vaccinations

In addition to a well-stocked first aid kit, it is important that both you and your horse or pony are up to date with vaccinations for tetanus (see page 168). Many puncture wounds that are a potential source of infection go unnoticed, so proper protection against this dangerous disease is very important. Check with your vet and your doctor.

First aid kit

- A list of key phone numbers, e.g. vet and insurance company
- Some paper and a pen
- A torch, ideally a small pen torch and a larger torch (with spare batteries)
- A thermometer
- A pair of curved stainless steel scissors
- A small pair of tweezers or forceps
- A clean bucket or big bowl
- Some antiseptic wound cleaner, e.g. povidone-iodine (pevidine®) or chlorhexidine (Hibiscrub®)
- An antiseptic spray
- Surgical spirit
- Petroleum jelly, e.g. Vaseline®
- Wound gel, e.g. Derma-gel®, Intrasite gel®, Nugel ®
- A range of dressings and bandages including those listed below
- Cotton wool
- Gamgee
- Ready-to-use poultice, e.g. Animalintex®
- Non-stick sterile dressing squares to go over wounds, e.g. melonin®
- Cotton stretch bandages, e.g. K band®
- Adhesive bandages, e.g. Elastoplast®
- Self-adhesive bandages, e.g. Vetrap®
- Zinc oxide tape or strong sticky tape
- Exercise bandages
- Stable bandages

Extras:
- Shoe removing kit
- Pliers and wire cutters
- Spare hoof pick
- Epsom salts
- Sterile saline bag to flush wounds
- Moist baby wipes to clean wounds
- Some sterile antiseptic impregnated nail brushes to clean wounds, e.g. E-Zscrub®
- Proprietary ice wrap or cooling bandage
- Clean old towels
- Bailer twine and some rope

Dealing with wounds

Wounds are the most common first-aid condition which every owner encounters with horses. Your immediate first aid aims should be to: prevent further injury, control blood loss, minimize contamination, and, finally, maintain cleanliness and thereby reduce the risk of any infection.

Contact your vet if:
- A wound is bleeding profusely.
- The horse is very lame, even if the wound itself is small.
- A wound is more than 5 cm (2 in) long and has gone right through the skin, so that it is gaping open and may need to be stitched by your vet.
- You suspect a foreign body in the wound.
- There is any suspicion that a vital structure, such as a joint, may be involved.
- The horse has NOT had an anti-tetanus vaccination.

Controlling bleeding

Remember that even a small amount of bleeding will look colossal when it is your favourite horse (or yourself). Just think of a spilt cup of coffee – it looks like a flood on the floor.

All but the most severe bleeding can be controlled by applying a clean, dry bandage pad with moderate pressure. If you are out in the middle of nowhere, sacrifice your T-shirt or whatever else is to hand to hold over the wound. If you can tape it in place or hold it there for at least five minutes, then it should allow blood clotting to occur.

The ideal is to use a sterile or, at least, a clean bandage to reduce any contamination by dirt and dust. However, you may not have one to hand, and you will have to utilize whatever is available to you. The three rules to remember when treating every wound are as follows.

1 Encourage clotting
First, you must stop the bleeding.

2 Check and clean the wound
Contamination and infection will both prevent wound healing. If an infection penetrates vital

structures, such as joints or tendon sheaths, a horse may be permanently crippled. It is vital to establish the position, depth and severity of any wound. You will need to clean the wound, so that you can see what is involved, provided that this can be done without making it bleed further.

3 Cover the wound

Cover the wound where possible to protect it. People often apply all sorts of potions and powders. However, remember that raw tissues are exposed, so never put anything on a wound which you would not put in your own eye.

Water-soluble wound gels

A useful new development in covering wounds is the water-soluble wound gels. Originally designed for human burns patients, they are also great for treating horses with wounds.

When they are applied to the area of damage, they help to keep a wound clean and moist. They will reduce the number of bacteria in the wound, bind bacterial toxins and speed up healing. They are an essential item in any horse owner's first-aid kit and a safe way of covering wounds.

Surgical skin staples

These are often used instead of stitching for certain skin wounds. They can be inserted quickly and are ideal when a horse does not want to stand still.

However, staples do not work well for jagged lacerations, or when the wound edges are under a lot of tension. All the same, they are often a way to repair clean cuts, such as head injuries.

Suturing a wound
This may be needed if:
• The edges are gaping.
• It is very large or deep.
• It is in an awkward place where it will scar. If you think a wound may need to be sutured, consult your vet as soon as possible, since it will heal more effectively if it is sutured whilst fresh. There is a six to eight hour optimum period for wound repair. Your vet will advise on the best course of action for any particular injury. Many wounds heal amazingly well without stitching.

Lameness

The horse's foot is the most common area of forelimb lameness.
It helps to understand the basic design of the equine foot
in order to avoid and treat the more common foot problems.

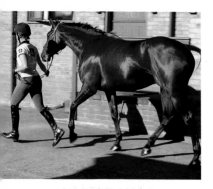

To detect signs of lameness ask someone to trot up your horse and study its movement closely for changes in its natural gait.

Wounds

The foot is vulnerable to penetrating wounds and infections, particularly as a horse is so heavy, with a relatively large weight on a small surface area. Also the hoof treads in dirty areas.

Anatomy of the foot

A horse's foot is composed of two-and-a-half bones:
- The third phalanx or coffin bone or the pedal bone.
- Half the second phalanx or the short pastern bone.
- The distal sesamoid or navicular bone.

The short pastern and coffin bones support the horse's weight while the navicular bone serves as a pivot for the deep digital flexor tendon. The joint between the first and second phalanges is the proximal interphalangeal or pastern joint, and the joint between the second and the third phalanges is the distal interphalangeal or coffin joint.

Soft tissue structures

As well as bones, there are numerous soft tissue structures including:
- The deep digital flexor tendon which runs down the back of the limb and angles around the navicular bone to attach to the back of the coffin bone.
- The navicular bursa is a fluid-filled pouch which sits between the navicular bone and the deep digital flexor tendon and helps cushion and protect the bone and tendon.
- The navicular bone also has three ligaments attaching it to the second and third phalanges.
- There are two large collateral ligaments attaching the second and third phalanges.

• Underneath the pedal bone is the digital cushion, a fibrous pad, which functions as a shock absorber.

External structures

There are also numerous key external structures of the foot, which are important for its overall health. The coronary band is where the skin and the hair intersect with the hoof wall. The hoof wall grows from the coronary band at a rate of 5–10 mm ($^1/_4$–$^1/_2$ in) per month. On the bottom of the foot are the sole, frog, white line and bars.

Preventing lameness

You can help prevent the possibility of lameness occurring in your horse by checking the feet regularly for any injuries, cracks in the wall of the hooves, bruising or thrush (infection of the frog). It is also very important to make sure that the horse is shod correctly with well-fitting shoes and that they are not left on for too long. A good diet and a well-drained, clean stable are also essential in preventing problems with the feet.

Lameness examination

If a horse remains lame, consult the vet or farrier. Most lameness is in the foot, and in many cases the farrier can solve it. However, if it persists, your vet will need to investigate with a comprehensive clinical examination including: palpation of the horse's limbs; checking the foot, including using a hoof-tester examination; joint manipulation; and examining the horse when it is moving to determine the severity of the lameness and which limb or limbs are affected.

Warning signs
A horse shifts its weight from foot to foot, rather than spreading it evenly. It may hold a front foot up or rest a foot when standing. Get someone to trot the horse in-hand on level, hard ground. Give the horse a little loose rein so it can move its head. A sound horse will hold its head level; if a foreleg is lame, it will nod its head. Watch the horse's hindquarters as they move. When the sound hindleg touches the ground, the hindquarter on that side dips, taking the weight.

Ask your vet
If you suspect laminitis in your horse or pony, you should contact your vet without delay as severe cases will need urgent treatment, and prompt action may help to reduce the severity. Chronic cases can benefit enormously from good farriery.

You should pick out your horse's feet twice every day to prevent thrush and other problems.

Laminitis (founder)

This is quite common in horses. There are two types:
● Acute laminitis is always treated as an emergency even if the horse or pony is in the early stages of the condition, as it may be reversible if treated promptly.
● Chronic laminitis is when the pedal bone has sunk or rotated. Such cases are not always an immediate emergency, but you should contact your vet.

The laminae are the lining tissues in the equine foot that connect the coffin bone to the inside of the hoof. Sensitive laminae cover the coffin bone and interlock with the insensitive laminae on the inside of the hoof wall. Generally, the laminae between the front edge of the coffin bone and the front hoof wall are the worst affected. As that area weakens, the deep digital flexor tendon continues to pull on the back of the pedal bone causing rotation of the bone.

If the entire foot is affected, the support for the pedal bone is compromised everywhere and the coffin bone sinks within the foot without rotation. This is the so-called 'sinker' – unusual but serious.

Signs of acute laminitis

● Lameness, especially when a horse is turning in circles, or shifting lameness when it is standing, or so much pain that it may not want to move at all.
● Hooves that feel hot and feet that are painful when pressure is applied to the sole.
● A raised pulse and respiratory rate, especially an increased digital pulse over the fetlock in all four feet.
● A stiff 'sawhorse stance', with the front feet stretched out in front to alleviate pressure on the toes, and the hind feet 'camped out'.
● The horse will move better on a soft surface.

• Occasionally, the hind feet are worse. Watch for horses shifting their weight from foot to foot.

Signs of chronic laminitis

• Recurrent lameness or feeling footsore, especially after trimming or on hard ground.
• Odd-looking feet with rings in the hoof wall that become wider as they are followed from toe to heel and a wider white line on the sole.
• Foot problems associated with bruised soles or recurrent abscesses.
• A thick, 'cresty' neck in a fat pony indicates a high risk of laminitis.

Preventing laminitis

Make sure you feed a good diet to your horse or pony. Avoid over-feeding, especially in spring and autumn when animals are susceptible to laminitis. If you need to slim your horse down, reduce the amount of concentrates in its diet and allow only limited grazing when grass is lush. Exercise it regularly and look after its feet, inspecting them daily for tell-tale signs. If in doubt, consult your vet immediately – don't delay until it is too late. Laminitis is always an emergency.

Treating laminitis

Your vet will have to identify the underlying cause. The horse or pony will need total box rest and must not be ridden; in severe cases, it should not be walked out. Keep it warm indoors in a clean stable with thick, soft bedding. You may also need to adjust its diet. Your vet will probably prescribe painkillers, anti-inflammatory drugs or even a mild sedative, and the feet should be trimmed by the farrier.

Common problems
Causes of lameness may include the following:
• **Pus in the foot. Horses can be so uncomfortable they can barely put the affected foot to the ground. See your farrier or vet as soon as possible.**
• **Bruising and lameness after shoeing, where a nail has pinched the sensitive tissues. Check with your vet or farrier.**
• **Navicular Disease. Poor foot conformation can lead to degenerative changes of the navicular bone and surrounding structures.Your vet and farrier will advise.**

Colic

Colic is any abdominal pain and can vary from a mild bout of discomfort that sorts itself out, to something more serious that requires medical treatment. Most dramatically, it can be a serious abdominal crisis requiring rapid skilled surgery.

What to look for

The majority of colic cases can be cured medically, but 5–10 per cent will need emergency surgery to survive. It is not possible to diagnose the cause purely on the basis of the horse's behaviour. Colic is always best controlled if the treatment is started early on. Regular checks on your horse will allow early detection of any problems.

Signs of colic

The signs of colic vary, but studies have shown that in horses with colic, 44 per cent roll; 43 per cent paw continuously or intermittently; 29 per cent lie down for long periods; 21 per cent get up and down; 14 per cent repeatedly look at their flank; 13 per cent curl their upper lip; 10 per cent back into a corner; 7 per cent kick at their abdomen; 4 per cent stand in a stretched position as if trying to pass urine; and 1 per cent fail to pass droppings for longer than 24 hours.

Often, the first clue you have that something is wrong with your horse is an unfinished feed, an untouched haynet or a churned-up bed. With severe colic, a horse can thrash around alarmingly and obviously will need urgent veterinary assistance. You should contact your vet if even mild colic signs persist for more than half an hour.

How often does it happen?
Colic is relatively common: studies have shown a background incidence of 0.1 to 0.2 episodes per horse per year. This means that if you have, say, 10 horses, you should expect one to two cases of colic per annum. Any more than this would be well worth discussing with your vet.

What to do

If colic is violent, the first essential thing that you must do is protect yourself against getting injured.

Try to calm the horse

Many horses will panic with the pain. Getting them up and walking on hard ground, e.g. concrete, where they are less likely to want to roll may help in the short term. If they are determined to go down, make sure that they have a big enough box with a deep bed, where they will not get cast.

Preventing injury

You must ensure also that the horse cannot get injured on stable fittings, such as mangers or buckets. You could remove them if they are not fixed or turn the horse out into a field or an arena, where it cannot damage itself. Although it is not ideal, rolling is unlikely to make the colic worse. By the time that the horse rolls, the guts may already be twisted and it is only nature's way of attempting to relieve the problem.

Warning

- It is wrong to walk a horse around for hours as this will only cause exhaustion. It should only be a stopgap whilst waiting for the vet.
- Remove all feed from within the horse's reach.
- Do not give any treatment, such as colic drenches, without consulting your vet first.
- Have some clean water, soap and a towel ready for the vet's arrival.
- Make sure you have transport available if the option of further treatment for the horse at an equine hospital is considered.

Surgery

At present, a horse with surgical colic will have about a 75 per cent chance of survival, provided you can get it to an equine hospital quickly and the surgery and aftercare are undertaken by an experienced team.

A horse that has been sick for a day before it reaches a clinic has a poorer chance of survival than one that is presented immediately. Many horses have undergone colic surgery and successfully returned to full work. It is well worth having insurance to cover the costs of any operation.

Caring for a sick horse

If your horse is unwell, then he will need your extra attention, especially if he is kept in a stable. Be vigilant and watch carefully for any changes in his demeanour or behaviour, and pay special attention to his comfort, diet and stable hygiene.

Some sick horses are kept inside their stable on box rest.

Box rest

Just as humans get tucked up into bed, sick horses may be confined to their stable. Box rest is useful for treating many conditions, especially lameness, but also following surgery.

Key care points

• Many lame horses need to be kept in, although they may not feel ill and will become bored.

• Regular grooming may help to keep them happy.

• You should choose their stable carefully: some horses like to watch activity around them while others are better somewhere quiet.

• Stabled horses that do not have access to grazing are more likely to develop stereotypical or abnormal behaviour, such as crib-biting, wind-sucking or weaving. Stable toys may help prevent this.

Feeding

It is necessary to cut the hard feed if a horse is kept in and is not being exercised. Change to a high-forage diet, so that he has plenty to munch, as eating keeps the horse occupied. Hay or short-chop forages that take longer to eat are better than haylage.

You should also be mindful of the fact that if a horse has no exercise and is fed high-energy feeds, it can develop muscle problems, which are known commonly as azoturia or 'tying-up'. Colic is another risk for horses stuck inside because of the change in their eating patterns, e.g. reduced grass intake will predispose them to constipation.

When a horse is kept in, count the droppings and if they reduce, you can feed a bran mash as a laxative. A one-off mash is a useful transition from a normal diet to convalescence rations. Frequent short walks to graze in-hand will help, if permitted as part of their treatment. Your vet will advise you.

Take care leading out

Always ensure when leading out your horse that it is adequately restrained. Even those horses that are normally relaxed may become difficult after being 'confined to barracks' for a while. If you are in doubt, use a bridle or a Chifney anti-rearing bit.

Watch for complications

A horse that is being box rested for severe lameness is at risk of damage to its legs as a result of their increased weight-bearing.
- You should check all the feet daily for any warning signs of laminitis, including increased warmth, digital pulses or soreness (see pages 180–181).
- A deep bed that encourages the horse to lie down will be helpful.
- The other legs should be support bandaged (see page 92). These bandages should include plenty of padding, and they should be checked regularly for bandage rubs.
- The legs should be massaged each time that the bandages are changed.

want to know more?
- Leaflets on essential health care, laminitis, colic, worm control and vaccinations can be obtained from the BHS
- For advice on weight loss plans, worm control, vaccinations and dental care, ask your vet
- For information on alternative medicine for horses, talk to your vet or you can contact the Association of Chartered Physiotherapists in Animal Therapy (ACPAT) on: www.acpat.org

weblinks
- Visit the BHS website at: www.bhs.org.uk
- Visit the British Equine Veterinary Association website at: www.beva.org.uk
- Visit the Farriers Registration Council website at: www.farrier-reg.gov.uk

Glossary

Action The movement of the horse's legs.

Backing The process of getting a horse accustomed to having a rider's weight on its back.

Bars The ends of the hoof wall, extending towards the centre of the sole from the heels.

Bars of the mouth Another term for the diastema, the space where the bit fits.

Bay Brown colour of the body with black mane, tail and lower legs.

Blaze A broad white stripe running down the face.

Brushing The knocking of one inside leg by its opposite number when the horse is moving.

Cantle The back of the saddle.

Cast When a horse is unable to get up and stand because it is stuck against a wall or a fixture in a loosebox.

Cast a shoe When a shoe comes off by accident.

Cavesson A piece of equipment used for lungeing a horse with rings to which the lunge line is attached.

Chaff Chopped straw or a straw/hay mix.

Chestnut Ginger-red colour of the body with similar or lighter mane and tail.

Clench The hook formed by the end of each horse shoe nail when it is bent over to hold it in place.

Cob A sturdy carrying-weight type of small horse, not exceeding 15.3 hh (155 cm).

Coldblood Applies to heavy workhorses, such as Shires, Percherons and Clydesdales.

Colic A painful stomach/bowel condition.

Colt An uncastrated male horse under four years of age.

Concentrates Types of food that are not roughage, e.g. cereals, legumes, lucerne hay or compound feeds, that are offered to provide high levels of nutrition – the additional energy part of the horse's ration.

Conformation The way a horse is put together. Conformation affects the horse's soundness, ability to perform and comfort to ride.

Crib-biting A stable 'vice' whereby a bored horse grabs hold of something and takes in air.

Croup The highest point on the horse's hindquarter.

Curb A type of bit with a strong effect on the horse.

Dam A horse's mother.

Dishing The front foot is thrown outwards, particularly in trot.

Dock The top of the tail that contains the bony vertebrae. Dorsal stripe A dark stripe along the back of a horse.

Dun Gold or cream body colour with black mane, tail and lower legs.

Entire A male horse that has not been castrated.

Fetlock The joint between the cannon bone and the long pastern bone.

Filly A female horse under four years of age.

Forging Hitting the underneath of the forefoot with the toe of the hind foot. You can hear a sound as it happens.

Frog The V-shaped pad on the sole of the hoof.

Gait The leg movement of a horse.

Gamgee A form of padding to go under bandages.

Gelding A castrated male horse of any age.

Grey A coat colour produced by a mixture of white and dark hairs.

Groove This may refer to the chin groove where the curb chain from a curd bit sits.

Gullet The channel underneath the seat of a saddle.

Half-bred A horse of whom one parent is a Thoroughbred.

Hand A unit of measurement for horses and ponies, equivalent to 10 cm (4 in).

Hock The joint in the middle of the back leg.

Hogged mane A mane that has been shorn down to the horse's neck.

Hotblood A horse bred from Thoroughbred or Arab stock.

Hunter A type and usually a half- or threequarter-bred animal, ranging from 15.3 hh (155 cm) upwards. Bred for stamina and jumping ability.

Knee rolls Front of the saddle flap the knees rest behind.

Laminitis A painful disease caused by the inflammation of tissues within the hoof. It can be recurrent.

Livery Rent-paid horse accommodation, sometimes with daily care included.

Lungeing A method of exercising a horse from on the ground whereby the horse moves around the handler on a long rein.

Manger A feed trough.

Mare A female horse of any age.

Near side The horse's left side.

New Zealand rug A tough waterproof rug for continuous use outdoors.

Numnah A wool or cotton pad used under the saddle to relieve pressure and absorb sweat, shaped to fit the saddle.

Off side The horse's right side.

Over-reaching The hind limb over-extends and the toe of the hind shoe strikes the forelimb.

Palomino A bright chestnut or gold body colour with a white mane and tail.

Pastern The part of the foot between the fetlock and the hoof.

Piebald Black and white patches on the coat.

Plaiting Also called lacing; at walk and trot the horse places one foot in front of the other.

Points of horse The names of each part of the horse.

Poll The point at the top of the head immediately behind the ears.

Polo pony A thoroughbred type under 16 hh (162 cm) with weight-carrying ability and suitable for adult riders.

Pommel The raised front of the saddle.

Pony A horse that is smaller than 14.2 hh (148 cm) when fully grown.

Rig A male horse that has one testicle retained in the abdomen.

Roan A mixture of white and other coloured hairs which are evenly distributed over the body.

Roller A broad strap around the belly to keep a rug in position. It must always be used with a wither pad.

Sire The father of a horse.

Skewbald Any other two-colour coat other than black and white.

Snaffle The commonest type of bit, usually with one ring on each side.

Sock White pastern and fetlock.

Sound horse A horse that is not lame.

Stallion An uncastrated male horse of any age.

Star A white patch on the forehead.

Staring coat A dull coat, often with the hairs standing up.

Stifle The joint where the hind leg appears to join the barrel.

Strawberry roan A pink-looking colour composed of a mix of chestnut and white hairs.

Stripe A narrow white marking down the face.

Surcingle A strap going round the belly to fix a rug in place. It should be used with a wither pad.

Tendon A gristly band of tissue that attaches a muscle to a bone.

Thoroughbred A horse that is registered in the General Stud Book and can trace its ancestry in the male line to three Arab stallions which were imported into Britain in the seventeenth and eighteenth centuries.

Toes turned out Horses that stand with either the forefeet or hind feet pointing outwards which usually brush their legs.

Tushes Teeth found in the mouths of male adult horses between the molars and the incisors.

Type Includes hunters, hacks, polo ponies and cobs. They are usually cross-breds and are distinguished from breeds as they are not registered in a stud book.

Vice A bad and undesirable habit.

Wall-eyed One or two blue eyes.

Warmblood A horse whose ancestry includes coldbloods and hotbloods. Used for riding or driving.

Weaving A stable 'vice' in which a bored, stabled horse rocks its head and neck from side to side stereotypically.

White line The junction between the insensitive and sensitive parts of the foot.

Whorls Changes in the direction of hair growth.

Wind The horse's breathing.

Withers The high point of the back, located at the base of the neck between the horse's shoulder blades.

Need to know more?

British Association of Homeopathic Veterinary Surgeons (The)
Chinham House
Standford in the Vale
Nr Faringdon
Oxon SN7 8NQ

British Dressage Ltd
National Agricultural Centre
Stoneleigh Park, Kenilworth
Warks CV8 2RJ
Tel: 024 7669 8830
Email: office@britishdressage.co.uk
Website: www.britishdressage.co.uk

British Driving Society
27 Dugard Place, Barford
Nr Warwick
Warks CV35 8DX
Tel: 01926 624420
Email: email@britishdrivingsociety.co.uk
Website: www.britishdrivingsociety.co.uk

British Equestrian Federation
National Agricultural Centre
Stoneleigh Park, Kenilworth
Warks CV8 2RH
Tel: 024 7669 8871
Email: info@bef.co.uk
Website: www.bef.org.uk

British Equine Veterinary Association
Wakefield House
46 High Street, Sawston
Cambs CB2 4BG
Tel: 01223 836970
Email: info@beva.org.uk
Website: www.beva.org.uk

British Horse Society (The)
Stoneleigh Deer Park
Kenilworth
Warks CV8 2XZ
Tel: 01926 707700
Email: enquiry@bhs.org.uk
Website: www.bhs.org.uk

British Show Jumping Association
National Agricultural Centre
Stoneleigh Park, Kenilworth
Warks
CV8 2RJ
Tel: 024 7669 8800
Email: bsja@bsja.co.uk
Website: www.bsja.co.uk

British Veterinary Association
7 Mansfield Street
London W1G 9NQ
Tel: 020 7636 6541
Email: bvahq@bva.co.uk
Website: www.bva.co.uk

Department for Environment, Food & Rural Affairs (DEFRA)
Nobel House
17 Smith Square
London SW1P 3JR
Helpline: 08459 335577
Email: helpline@defra.gsi.gov.uk
Website: www.defra.gov.uk

National Association Farriers & Blacksmiths
Avenue B, 10th Street
National Agricultural Centre
Stoneleigh Park, Kenilworth
Warks CV8 2LG
Tel: 024 7669 6595
Email: nafbae@nafbae.org.uk
Website: www.nafbae.org.uk

Pony Club (The)
National Agricultural Centre
Stoneleigh Park, Kenilworth
Warks CV8 2RW
Tel: 024 7669 8300
Email: enquiries@pcuk.org
Website: www.pcuk.org

Royal College of Veterinary Surgeons
Belgravia House
62–64 Horseferry Road
London SW1P 2AF
Tel: 020 7222 2001
Email: admin@rcvs.org.uk
Website: www.rcvs.org.uk

Society of Master Saddlers (UK) Ltd
Green Lane Farm, Green Lane
Stonham, Stowmarket
Suffolk IP14 5DS
Tel: 01449 711642
Email: enquiries@mastersaddlers.co.uk
Website: www.mastersaddlers.co.uk

Worshipful Company of Farriers
19 Queen Street
Chipperfield, Kings Langley
Herts WD4 9BT
Tel: 01923 260747
Email: theclerk@wcf.org.uk
Website: www.wcf.org.uk

Worshipful Company of Saddlers
Saddlers' Hall
40 Gutter Lane
Cheapside
London EC2V 6BR
Tel: 020 7726 8663
Email: clerk@saddlersco.co.uk

Further reading

The BHS Directory of Where to Ride, Train and Stable Your Horse (The British Horse Society)
The BHS Instructors' Manual for Teaching Riding, Islay Auty FBHS (The British Horse Society)
The BHS Manual of Equitation, Consultant Editor Islay Auty FBHS (The British Horse Society)
The BHS Manual of Stable Management, Consultant Editor Islay Auty FBHS (The British Horse Society)
The BHS Riding and Road Safety Manual: Riding and Roadcraft (The British Horse Society)
The BHS Training Manual for Progressive Riding Tests 1–6, Islay Auty FBHS (The British Horse Society)
The BHS Training Manual for Stage 1, Islay Auty FBHS (The British Horse Society)

The BHS Training Manual for Stage 2, Islay Auty FBHS (The British Horse Society)
The BHS Training Manual for Stage 3 and PTT, Islay Auty FBHS (The British Horse Society)
The BHS Veterinary Manual, P. Stewart Hastie MRCVS (The British Horse Society)
Driver Licensing Information pamphlet (The Stationery Office)
Driving, The Official Driving Test and The Highway Code (available from bookshops)
Learn to Ride, Islay Auty (The British Horse Society)
Pony Handbook, David Taylor BVMS, FRCVS, FZS (HarperCollins)
Riding and Roadcraft (The British Horse Society)

The British Horse Society

The British Horse Society was founded in 1947 and has become a world-leading authority on both horse welfare and rider safety. Membership currently stands at almost 63,000. In addition, there are 38,000 members of affiliated Riding Clubs.

As a registered charity, membership is vitally important to the BHS. Subscriptions provide the money that enables the charitable objectives of the Society to be met: promoting the welfare, care and use of horses and ponies, through the encouragement of good horsemanship and the improvement of horse care and breeding.

Index

○ **Collins** need to know?

Look out for these recent titles in Collins' practical and accessible need to know? series.

  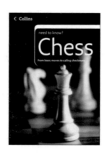 

Aquarium Fish — Card making — Chess — First Aid

Horse and Pony Care — Latin Dancing — Mushroom Hunting — NLP

Outdoor Survival — Party Games — Universe — Weather Watching

Other titles in the series:

Antique Marks
Birdwatching
Body Language
Buying Property in France
Buying Property in Spain
Card Games
Children's Parties
Codes & Ciphers
Decorating
Digital Photography
DIY

Dog Training
Drawing & Sketching
Dreams
Golf
Guitar
How to Lose Weight
Kama Sutra
Kings and Queens
Knots
Low GI/GL Diet
Pilates

Poker
Pregnancy
Property
Speak French
Speak Italian
Speak Spanish
Stargazing
Watercolour
Weddings
Wine
Woodworking

The World
Yoga
Zodiac Types

To order any of these titles, please telephone **0870 787 1732** quoting reference **263H**.
For further information about all **Collins** books, visit our website:
www.collins.co.uk